THE POETRY OF FRANCIS WEBB

Piercing into the Psyche

Rodolfo Delmonte

Copyright © 2023 Rodolfo Delmonte
Copyright © 2023 Generis Publishing

All rights reserved. This book or any portion thereof may not be reproduced or used in any manner whatsoever without the written permission of the publisher except for the use of brief quotations in a book review.

Title: **THE POETRY OF FRANCIS WEBB**

Piercing into the Psyche

ISBN: 979-8-88676-898-5

Author: Rodolfo Delmonte

Cover image: Personal Image

Publisher: Generis Publishing
Online orders: www.generis-publishing.com
Contact email: info@generis-publishing.com

THE POETRY OF FRANCIS WEBB

Piercing into the Psyche

Rodolfo Delmonte

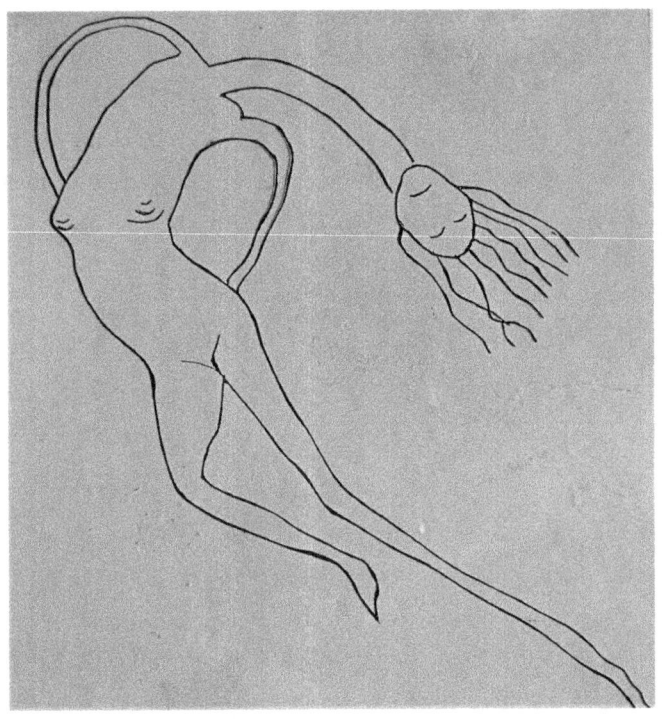

*With a Foreword by Christ Wallace Crabbe
And a Computational and Quantitative Analysis*

Cover drawing by an unknown schizophrenic artist - shown at the Documentary Exhibition - Psychiatric Hospital Udine - Italy

PREFACE TO 2ND EDITION

I decided to reprint and reedit the first edition of this book for a number of reasons. The first one and most important is the renewed interest in Francis Webb's poetry ensued as a result of the re-edition of his Collected Poems by Toby Davidson in 2011. The second is as much important as the first one and is a formal one: the first edition was published on the basis of sheets of paper typed on my typewriter and there was no wordprocessor with an automatic corrector to check for possible typos. So this is a way to improve both on the overall printing outlook and on the text.

There are then important additions:

- first of all, the chapters have section subtitles to guide the reader;
- the Introduction has been turned into Chapter I and two sections have been added;
- the previous final chapter has been totally erased and transformed into a section of Chapter V
- a new chapter - Chapter VI - has been added with computational analysis (computers at the time were very different!!), producing among other things, impressive graphical representations of combined comparisons between Webb's poetry and a number of contemporary important poets.

FOREWORD

The poetry of Francis Webb is one of the most remarkable, intense and unshakably genuine bodies of literary testimony to have come out of Australia in its short and the most part extroverted history. This poetry, inward and deeply, richly verbal, was the essential mode of self-knowledge lifelong for a man who never found self-knowledge, or any other kind of knowledge, easy to come by. Webb had no tool other than his poetry with which to probe the threats and paradoxes of his world, a world which was for a paranoid schizophrenic constantly beating and battering in at all the portals of knowledge. The marvel is that in the long torment of his life this modest, threatened man went on producing poetry of such distinction, such richly orchestrated verbal intensity. Even at the very end, after long silence, he could surface again with "Lament for St Maria Goretti", not one of his best poems to be sure, but still the utterance of a person for whom the verbal art was the one genuine quest for truth, all else being what the poet calls "Nothing scrambling ashore".

Despite the fervent advocacy of Sir Herbert Read, Webb's poetry remains all too little known outside Australia: it is certainly not known in New York, where the reputations in English letters are made and broken these days. But this is the common measure for a writer who comes from the cultural outskirts and not from the imperium, the heartland. And Webb himself would have expected such neglect: he would have expected some silent conspiracy or other to shut him out from any glory except for that portion which still, he believed, fell upon him from Christ's incarnation. For Webb was atypical of mid-twentieth century poets in that he had learned his art from some of the craggiest and most despairing modern masters but could still turn gladly to the simple truths enshrined in the figures of the Christ child and St Francis of Assisi.

It is strange to come to such realizations, but I find that I have now been reading Francis Webb's poetry for almost thirty years. After his sturdy, Browningesque first volume, *A Drum for Ben Boyd*, which had not made a deep impression on me, I happened on his slim volume, *Birthday*, in a narrow Melbourne bookshop and was immediately enraptured by the dense musicality of his language, by the sense of something rich and strange which had now come into Australian poetry and which persuaded me, in turn, how profoundly serious an art the craft of verse could be. To cite just one example, "Dawn Wind on the Islands", from *Leichhardt in Theater*, creates islands of language which are strangely more real than any merely physical islands could continue to be: the drugged yet supple language of that poem builds an image or entity which memory cannot set aside, so vivid is it.

Again and again in Webb's books, early and late, I was attracted by the immense linguistic flexibility, or a kind which betokens great strain at the same time, by the indecorous rapidity with which the language could move from metaphor to metaphor, tone to ton e; there was a kind of wit, but not an urbane wit, in his strenuous attempts to take the whole globe of language for his province. His best poems can modulate rapidly all the way from the kind of diction that goes with a clever elegance – not at all a quality one would have associated with Webb the man – to a passionately expressionist language, "bred in the bone". There is great speed and richness in his marshalling of inner and outer perceptions. Often its method is that of unashamed catachresis.

The ever-present life of Francis Webb's verse is registered very much in the verbs, which are highly active, challenging, tangential, changing, the movement of one another. For instance, four consecutive lines in "Banksia" begin with the verbal forms, "Munching ...

Shambles ... Picking up ... Girt ...", each line a new lunge, a new beginning, while a later stanza tries to contain the incompatible activities of "creeps", "lull", "rock", "maul", "thump" and "looted". All is dramatic. Things move, things generate others, things react against one another: there is no principle of peace, nor even of stasis. It is in this active presentation of psychomachia that we find Webb's great relevance to a new generation of poets, those for whom the very notions of self and order and discourse are psychological absurdities, falsely dependent on pre-Freudian notions of the self's integrity. For all his Christian faith, he could never reduce or simplify the mysteries. As in a late poem, "Gustav Mahler", he always felt, desperately felt that "We slaver wonder at the touch and taste/Of your great swaying themes". He never imposed false conclusions on the perpetual conflict of the senses.

Dr Delmonte is the first critic of the poetry to have given due weight to the topography of the psychological condition which lay behind him. We can never come to any true understanding of Webb's poetry unless we confront that difficult terrain and this is what he has sought to do. His psychological questionings will profoundly deepen our sense of what Webb's poems really are; for the blanket term, poetry, or literature, spreads over many different kinds of manifestation, attempting to squeeze them into the one mould. It is my belief that this book will substantially aid our understanding of the modes in which Francis Webb bore witness to his divided self and to his sacral world.

Chris Wallace-Crabbe

[this Foreword has been reported as it was originally written in 1977]

CONTENTS

PREFACE TO 2ND EDITION 7

FOREWORD 9

CHAPTER I: POETRY, MADNESS, AND METAPHORS 15

   1.1 A Double Personality: Poet and Outcast.................................... 15

   1.2 Psychoanalysis and Creativity 21

   1.3 Webb's Poetic Language 24

   1.4 Schizophrenic Language 28

   1.5 Allegories and Symbols 37

CHAPTER II: THE ALIENATED IDENTITY 47

   2.1 The early poems 47

   2.3 The Quest for a Metaphysical Dimension 64

CHAPTER III: TOWARDS THE CREATION OF A PERSONAL MYTH 75

   3.1 The sacred illness and the Myth of Christ 75

   3.2 The union of the opposites with Christ 82

   3.3 The opposites and immanence 86

   3.4 Doctors and Judges, Sin and Guilt 91

   3.5 Myth of Christ and Sexual Imagery 97

CHAPTER IV: THE STRUGGLE FOR SURVIVAL 107

   4.1 The Artist as a Christ-Figure 107

   4.2 The Ward and the Poet-Patient-Fool 111

   4.3 The Ward as a Prison 114

   4.4 The Mother and the Return into the Womb 121

4.5 A Short Introduction to Chapter V and VI 124

CHAPTER V: A QUANTITATIVE ANALYSIS OF LINGUISTIC DEVIATION 127

5.2 Semiotics and feedback devices 129

5.3 Poetry as deviation from the norm 131

5.4 Quantitative Lexical Comparison with W.B.Yeats and American Norm 132

5.5 A comparative quantitative analysis of Vocabulary Richness. 139

CHAPTER VI: COMPUTATIONAL ANALYSIS OF WEBB'S CORPUS 151

6.1 SPARSAR - Automatic Analysis of Poetic Structure and Rhythm with Syntax, Semantics and Phonology 151

6.2 Related Work and State of the Art 155

6.3 Rhetoric Devices, Metrical and Prosodic Structure 168

6.5 Computing Phonetic and Prosodic Structure 182

6.6 SPARSAR Linguistic and Statistic Graphical Modeling 185

   6.6.1 *Comparing two poets: Webb and Plath* *188*

   6.6.2 *Comparing Webb with more poets* *193*

BIBLIOGRAPHY 207

On Poetry 207

On Literature, Myth, Symbolism, Anthropology 208

On Psychology and Creativity 210

Computational and Quantitative Linguistics 212

Articles on Francis Webb 221

CHAPTER I: POETRY, MADNESS, AND METAPHORS

1.1 A Double Personality: Poet and Outcast

Francis Webb, now celebrated as the Australian poet's poet has been left totally forgotten for almost 40 years after his death and the first commemorative seminar held at the University of Sydney in 1974. This is what Chris Wallace Crabbe holds in the Foreword reported here without modifying it in any word. The reality now is quite different, and this is certified by Toby Davidson, the editor of the fortunate new version of Webb's *Collected Poems*. According to Davidson, the book has been disseminated and sold all over the world and Francis Webb now is present in a conspicuous number of website dedicated to his poetry. But what really matters is the fact that now he has become the national poet most celebrated and read at all levels from school to TV and theater. in Webb"s home city of Sydney in particular[1], Webb is not only loved but *lived* by whole networks of families and friends who recite and discuss his works well apart from any ambition to be „literary".[2]

Robert Adamson's first lesson of his Chair of Poetry at UTS, entitled "Something Absolutely Splendid", looked closely at the life and work of Francis Webb and discussed how he influenced his first book. Michael Griffith attending the lesson commented:

"Adamson spoke eloquently and passionately about Webb's importance to continuing generations of Australian poets about the fierce originality of his language and the breadth of his

---

[1] There's an annual reading of Francis Webb poetry organized by Poetry Australia since Toby Davidson published the revised edition of his Collected Poems, it may be found here: https://www.australianpoetry.org/rea dings-events-and-launches/7th-annual-francis-webb-reading/
[2] Toby Davidson, 2012. *Breath, Laughter, Creation*: Launches, Reviews And Errata For Francis Webb *Collected Poems*

mind breaking through barriers of personal suffering and engaging creativity with a vast array of subjects: mental illness, Australian exploration, music and the natural landscape."

Michael Griffith[3] was one of the participants in the first public tribute to Francis Webb after his death. The Seminar to Commemorate Francis Webb was held in the Western Tower of the University of Sydney and was organized by the members of the English Department in May 13-14, 1974. The other participants were: Douglas Stewart, R.D.Fitzgerald, Judith Wright, Rosemary Dobson, David Campbell, G.A.Wilkes, Vincent Buckley, R.F.Brissenden, Chris Wallace Crabbe, H.F.Heseltine, Robert Adamson, Sister Mary Francisca, W.D.Ashcroft, Rodney Hall and James Tulip. There were readings from Collected Poems, and Recordings of Francis Webb which made almost everybody cry. There were also the sisters of the poet, Claudia Snell and Mrs. Leonie Meere. I was also invited and was somewhat shocked at the experience: I was just arriving from Europe and my plans were a Ph.D. on Patrick White. But Chris Wallace Crabbe and Philip Martin, my mentors and thesis supervisor warmly offered – and strongly advised me – to work on poetry. Of course I loved poetry but didn't know much about Australian poetry. Besides, my work on Patrick White's highly elaborate prose style and language, was regarded a sufficient guarantee of success. The poets included Webb, so I was asked to take part in the seminar. After the Seminar, I developed the necessary empathy with the poet and his work to make it the most important chapter of my thesis and to continue writing afterwards, back in Europe, with the same enthusiasm.

Francis Webb is famous for his language and the way in which he treats words and phrases as Vincent Buckley wrote in his essay 'A Poet

---

[3] Michael has a website dedicated to Francis Webb with a lot of information. It also features Seminars dedicated to the poetry. This is the link, https://michaelgriffith1.com/tag/gods-fool, and in general, https://michaelgriffith1.com/category/francis-webb/

of Harmony':

> "He was a great phrase maker and there are phrases, sentences, cadences in poem after poem that are quite unforgettable. He was a great master, and sometimes a victim, of metaphor, the most metaphor addicted poet in this country, I would say, and it is noticeable that time and time again the energy of those very ample driving rhythms is also the energy with which metaphors are picked up, created and extended through the stanza."

At the Francis Webb Commemorative Seminar held at the University of Sydney in May, 1974, Webb's poetic work was discussed as the product of a genius, a great poet, or a saintly man: nobody mentioned the fact that Webb the man had spent 22 years of his life in mental hospitals, eventually labelled as paranoid schizophrenic, and that his illness led to his premature and untimely death.

A passing allusion was made by Rosemary Dobson, but only as a pitiable biographical accident, which had obviously nothing to do with his poetic achievements. What these people have tried to do is splitting Webb into two different entities: the poet, and the man – mentally ill – as if they were not one and the same person. My analysis of Webb's work is based on two premises: I intend to take his mental illness into account and detect the possible causes that turned him into a mentally ill person as long as this is borne out by his poetry. For this reason I devoted a lot of space to the study of his poetic language, together with the biographical traits of his life which may be relevant to try to clarify possible relations with his poetic work. It is however important to note that in the first years after the appearance of the disease at the age of 24 there was no consensus on the diagnosis as reported by Toby Davidson[4].

---

[4] The Master and the Mask: Francis Webb's Verse Biography, 2016, in *Biography*, University of Hawaii Press, Vol.39:1, p.47

He received a series of different diagnoses including "persecution mania". The consensus on the mental illness as paranoid schizophrenia only came after 1960.

In Webb's poetry it is possible to find two main themes: the first and most important one is the identity problem, in social and existential terms. This will be explored by a psychological analysis developed partly on the basis of biographical data available and also as a result of talking to people involved, who knew Webb personally, including doctors. The second theme is complementary to the first and converges on the myth of Christ.

What we know from the approach taken by literary critics like Lionel Trilling[5], is as follows:

> "The myth of the sick artist... has established itself because it is of advantage to the various groups who have one or another relation with art....The connection between art and mental illness has been formulated not only by those who are openly or covertly hostile to art, but also and more significantly by those who are more intensely partisan to it... accepting the idea that his illness is a condition of the artist's power to tell the truth"

> But there is another group which is more important to my argument: the religious and clerical society who contributed, particularly in a later phase of Webb's life, to create the myth. These people regarded his as a saint, overlooking the fact that he was made to die of a "saintly" mental illness in "lagers" [German word for concentration camps], which were mental hospital at the time.

In this case, the supporters of the theory that suffering has to

---

[5] In The Liberal Imagination – Essays on Literature and Society, 1979, Peregrine Books, p.166.

be regarded as a precondition to attain spiritual illumination, or as Trilling puts it "..the artist derived his authority from the knowledge gained through suffering" [ibid.,172].

But if it is true that Webb ended his life as a schizophrenic, he like Van Gogh, was both mentally ill and an artist: in other words, he was an artist not "in spite of" his illness, nor "thanks" to it. Schizophrenia is as much part of Webb's poetic development as any other philosophical, religious and ideological issue. Any etiology (and ideology) of Webb's mental illness is, in my opinion, linked to two important facts in his terrible childhood: the death of his mother when he was two and a half years of age, followed by his father's decision to send him at the age of three to live with his grandparents. The loss of his mother, and the subsequent dislocation of his affections to a different person, could well have prevented him from developing a strong and secure ego and could be regarded as one cause of his so-called mental illness.

There are at least two other cases of famous poets who underwent medical treatment and had a similar life-story: Gérard de Nerval, who lost his mother at the age of two and was raised by his uncle; and Stéphane Mallarmé, who lost his mother at the age of five and lived with his grandparents[6] – but also Ezra Pound and Alan Ginsberg were both hospitalized for a substantial period of time the second but for a long period the first.

These biographical facts are obviously to be taken only as hints: it might well be the case that Webb found in his grandparents a proper substitute for his parents' affections. According to Freud's theories, Webb's mother died when he was entering the phallic or genital phase, and when he had to deal with the Oedipus complex. The disappearance of the father, who died when he was nine, has also to be regarded as an

---

[6] E.Erikson, 1968, Identity and Crisis, New York; Charles Mauron, 1963. Des métaphores obsédantes au mythe personnel, Paris

important fact psychologically speaking: in Freudian terms, this fact might have disturbed a proper sexual and libidinal discharge. A consequence to this would be the hindrance of a regular entrance into society caused by feelings of guilt and inferiority complexes, which stifle the strength of purpose as well as a proper channeling of initiatives.

In this way, instead of developing a feeling of confidence in himself as a participant in a community of men, Webb might have been led to developing feelings of extraneousness from and unfitness for society. In psycho-analytic words, the function of his Super-Ego, and the Oedipus complex, will not be developed properly: the latency period, extending from three and a half years of age to the onset of puberty is the period in which – always according to psycho-analytical theories[7] – the child most needs the mother, to learn how to direct his affections, and the father, in order to be reassured about his sexual role, hence his social role. For instance, the first part-object experienced by the child is the breast and, according to Melanie Klein's theories[8], this can be "good" "bad" or "ideal": every child goes through a schizo-paranoid and a depressive position according to its relationship with the mother's breast or the father's penis.

The theories of such a post-Freudian as Winnicott reduce the problem of schizoid personalities to the "good mother" and the "bad mother". When a child has a good infancy experience, that is, when his relations to his mother are natural, in accordance with the "feminine" role of the mother, who has to provide the child with security and a sense of symbiosis with the world, then the child will eventually "introject"[9] the mother (or the breast), the female aspect of the psyche.

---

[7] D.W.Winnicott, 1958, Collected Papers: Through Pediatrics to Psycho-Analysis, London
[8] Melanie Klein, *The Collected Writings of Melanie Klein* - Volume 2 – *The Psychoanalysis of Children*, London: Hogarth Press
[9] "introjection" is the process of absorbing the superego from the parents; in J.P.Chaplin, 1971. Dictionary of

By "carrying" always his mother within himself, the individual is able to cope with society; if this condition fails, the would-be man develops feeling of anxiety, of insecurity, hence psychosis[10].

Besides, simply the fact of Webb being an introverted individual, sexually and socially insecure, could also lead to the conclusion that he was, psycho-analytically speaking, a potential schizoid or psychotic[11]. Furthermore, to make it more complicated, Fairbairn maintains that potentially everyone is a schizoid[12].

1.2 Psychoanalysis and Creativity

When these theories are applied to the creative individual, they become a justification of his condition in society. In fact, nobody has yet been able to come to terms with the core, the essence of the creative impulse; the "divine" spark remains ultimately an inexplicable phenomenon[13]. What emerges from a general survey of psycho-analytical theories on the creative personality is that the creative act, since it has to be elaborated in isolation by an individual who, from Romanticism onward, sets himself against the canons established by society, and whose personality is basically preoccupied with his innermost reactions, is closely linked with an idiosyncratic structure of the psyche, if not with sickness[14].

This approach is particularly true with Jungian theorizers: in his

---

Psychology, New York
[10] See Andrew Crowcroft, 1968. The Psychotic, Understanding Madness, Penguin Books
[11] See Harry Guntrip, 1968. Schizoid Phenomena, Object-Relations and the Self, London
[12] W.R.D. Fairbairn, 1952, Psychoanalytic Studies of the Personality, London
[13] See Antony Storr, 1972. The Dynamics of Creation, New York
[14] See among others, Roger Fry, 1924. The Artist and Psycho-analysis, London; Ernst Kris, 1953, Psycho-analytic Exploration in Art, London; Edmund Bergler, 1950, The Writer and Psycho-analysis, New York; Janine Chasseguet-Smirgel, 1971. Pour une psychoanalyse de l'art et de a créativité, Paris; Octave Mannoni, 1969. Clefs pour l'Imaginaire ou l'Autre Scène, Paris

essay on creativity, Erich Neumann gives a portrait of the creative artist, which borders on the Promethean figure: "The creative artist, whose mission it is to compensate for consciousness and the cultural canon, is usually an isolated individual, a hero who must destroy the old in order to make possible the dawn of the new."[15] And further on "the modern artist...[is] an outsider in society, he stands alone, delivered over to the creative impulse in himself"[ibid.p.96]. In his essay "Creative Man and Transformation" he argues on the connection between the creative impulse and the necessity to encompass suffering and sickness, and we report a long citation which serves our argument perfectly:

> "In the creative individual, regardless of biographical details, reductive analysis will almost invariably discover mother-fixation and parricide, i.e. Oedipus complex: "family romance", i.e. the search for the unknown father, and narcissism, i.e. preservation of a relation to himself in opposition to love of the environment and of the outside object. This relation of the creative man to himself involves an enduring and insuperable paradox. This type's innate receptivity makes him suffer keenly from his personal complexes. But from the very outset this suffering, because he always experiences his personal complexes along with their archetypal correspondences, is not only a private and personal suffering but at the same time a largely unconscious existential suffering... Consequently, the individual history of every creative man is always close to the abyss of sickness; he does not, like other men, tend to heal the personal wounds involved in all development by an increased adaptation to the collectivity. His wounds remain open, but his suffering from them is situated depths from which another curative power

---

[15] Erich Neumann, 1959. Art and the Creative Unconscious, Four Essays, London, p.94

arises, and this curative power is the creative process."
[Ibid.,pp.185-6]

So, if the Freudians speak in terms of sublimation and of fixation with an infantile stage in the development of the personality, the Jungian discourse is mere tautology: since creativity makes a man different from his fellowmen, it entails suffering and sometimes sickness, creation becomes the only cure. All these partial and somewhat general expositions of psycho-analytical and psychological theories could well be applied to Webb's case: but in Webb's life there is a point of no return, where a complete regression takes place, which hinders a sound creative expression and leads eventually to his death as a paranoid schizophrenic.

Besides these theories do not take into account another important factor: both the so-called "mental illness" and the works of art are the manifestation of an anthropological condition, that is a condition which springs from its cultural and historical inner situation, which continually shifts in time, and which rejects any possibility of a norm imposed from the outside, and is represented by the society and that portion of the society that makes up his environment. The "us" and "them" can thus be interchanged without reaching any feasible solution to the survival of the individual's personality.

Most of Webb's poetry is directed towards this aim: almost all of it is structures on a dialectical basis. Its central myth, the myth of Christ, is used as a mediator between opposite poles: the whole of Webb's life has been a quest for harmony, order and balance in his psychic world. The archetypal symbol of Christ is the key to the understanding of Webb's mythopoiesis: Christ the mediator, the god become man, is the pivot of Webb's poetic creativity. It provides Webb with the means to endorse the conflict of opposed forces in the heart of his being.

In Webb's work, the search for a metaphysical dimension is envisaged in terms of immanence: that is, he does not try to solve the dilemma of man's existence in terms of a return to an Edenic state, a retreat into nature outside civilization. He could not escape, since he suffered the condition of the stigmatized person rejected by his society and compelled to live in ghettos, where human beings are made to lose progressively their identity, let alone their dignity. He rather devotes himself to representing the life of alienated individuals so that the poetic creation acquires a cathartic function, redeeming his "guilt", his sin of being different, and the sins of society.

1.3 Webb's Poetic Language

Webb's use of poetic language is very revealing. He does not resort to dogmatic views or orthodox religious clichés, he rather finds and develops a new language, a new poetic lexicon which revitalizes the old formulas. His poetic language also reflects his view of reality. In Webb's language reality is characterized as a compound of opposite forces intertwined in the dialectical and evolving structure of the poems. There is a perennial labouring towards an ultimate illumination where the duality is encompassed in its twofold aspect. Life is envisaged as a continual struggle, a coacervate of opposite forces, a combination of disparate elements. In this way Webb affirms that there is no prefixed pattern in which reality can be included, no fixed formula: his poems are an all-comprehensive pattern, moving continually from one pole to another, swaying from one tension to another and creating new conflicts inside their structure.

Here lies Webb's modernity: it can be detected in his rejection of a fixed point of reference, of a coherent organization of the real on a linguistic level. The contemporary mode of semantic and syntactic linguistic organization of reality does not lend itself to many positive hypotheses: the interdependence of linguistic and structural elements links the dissolution of a middle-class organic realism to the collapse of a rational and unifying interpretation of the world. With Webb we pass from the one-dimensional society that more traditional Australian poets like A.D.Hope and James McAuley portray, to the endorsement of the alienation and of the "difference" of the individual. Webb does not use Christ as a reductive symbol: he rather broadens its valence, until he makes it an all-embracing myth.

In Hope and McAuley the complete lack of experiment and complexity in the language, the linearity of syntactic and grammatical structures, bear upon their vision of life: their "Weltanschaung" reveals no exterior conflict, no apparent dichotomies between man and society. It is a positivist, realistic view of the world which affirms that man can master his world through reason and that reality is plain and there is no incongruity in man's condition. In both poets, man is fully in harmony with his environment and society, where he can find his right position: or rather that society can be changed or influenced by the poet, who can impose his views on it because he is acknowledged by the rest of the community of which he is an integrating and important part. It is a society which has given him respect and self-confidence.[16]

Particularly in "Socrates" Webb realizes, as we shall see, the complete passage from the descriptive or discursive mode into the identifying asyndeton, or the metaphor "tout court", which is typical of the poetic exclusion, of the suppression of any realistic remainder. Buckley's affirmation that Webb was a "great master, the most metaphor-addicted poet in his country"[17] needs elucidation.

---

[16] See R.Delmonte, 1977. Myth, Creativity and Society in the Poetry of James McAuley, A.D.Hope, Francis Webb, unpublished Ph.D. Dissertation, Monash University, English Dept.
[17] Vincent Buckley, "A Poetry of Harmony", *Poetry Australia,* No. 56, September, (1975), p.39

Metaphor is basically a creative utterance, a manifestation of creativity; it has a psychological reality in that it prefigures a whole vision of the world, which can be paraphrased in a peculiar way in order to perceive the object in its uniqueness, in its originality, by a syncretic fusion with it, and with the precise aim of participating in all its characters. It represents an approach to reality and a conception of one's own Ego in relation to this reality and to the Ego of others. It is a means of communication, but it also captures new individual values. This is because metaphor is not merely a semantic transposition, a transference of meaning, but dissociates it to form a new one; it reconciles two poles: subjective/objective, interior/exterior. Metaphors stem from the need to reconcile a conflict; they can also been regarded as a cognitive means to express reality, alternative to the one based on the rational/logical/conventional mode.

The spate of metaphors in Webb's word is a sign of his strongly felt need to master his interior and exterior conflicts mirroring his condition in society and other human beings' similar conditions. Since metaphors answer to the unbalance between interior and exterior reality, they unconsciously satisfy the needs of the former reality, when the latter has failed to realize them. In this sense metaphors, in a later phase of Webb's work, stem from the unbalance created by his life as a prisoner of the institution – his internal needs – and the society of "normal" people – the external needs. But metaphors can also become a substitute for the exterior reality – and this is the "victim"-like aspect of Webb's metaphoric mania. If one keeps on seeing an object different from what it is, one can come to the point of not seeing any longer what it really is. If the primary function of metaphor is that of externalizing and making communicable the interior clusters of sensations and emotions, one could reach the point of annihilating the exterior reality which is the first cause of conflicts in Webb's psyche.

And, as we shall see, Webb at a certain point stops fitting his interior reading of reality into the exterior. Nonetheless, if the basis of metaphor is a conflict between interior and exterior contents of the psyche, there always has to be a certain availability in letting the interior be pierced by the exterior and vice-versa: this disposition will always be Webb's peculiar trait, at least until his silence, the one that will save him from locking himself up in the world of madness.

But when is a poem really worth reading? We know that a poem is such when it does not just "tell" us something but it "suggests", by stimulating our imagination, a feeling, an emotion, while at the same time remaining anchored in reality, in real experience. To illustrate this concept, I will use a quotation on poetry by Christopher Brennan, that is explaining more than any word and has been used by Chris Wallace Crabbe in his book "Read it Again":

> Let us then say that poetry is the expression of imagination in language, acknowledging that this is not a definition, but a text for explanation. Imagination, then, as manifested in art, is a perceptive act; the perception of analogies and correspondences, whereby things which in ordinary consciousness led a separate existence are fused into unity, so that sensuous facts become symbols. (by Christopher Brennan, quoted by C.W.C., ibid. 12)

In other words a poet – as Webb did in his poetry – while describing a real experience, which may also encompass ideas and abstract worlds, at the same time suggests or inspires feelings and emotions. The poet in fact wants us to share these feeling in order to conceptualize the poem in another level of consciousness, a metalevel. This is usually done through a careful usage of words and their meaning, or perhaps I should say by the "transposition" of their meaning in a metalevel, the one wrought especially for the reader in the poem, by means of rhetorical devices and carefully structured syntactic constructions. In this we agree with Lyn Jacobs' remarks in her review of "Socrates": what is relevant is "Webb's investigation of the relation of world and word and recognition of language as a conceptual structure, artifact and tool of the prevailing culture". Webb's poetry is intense, complex, sometimes "unfathomable" as T.Davidson comments in his preface to the Collected Poems[18].

Also revealing are comments by Tina Giannoukos: "Throughout his work Webb's language is intricately rich, not with empty verbal play, but in the sense that it gestures constantly to the sublime tension of living, not as a burden, but as a profound obligation"; and elsewhere "Even at its most dense his language retains its suppleness. Webb should be read out loud for the musicality of his language which never overwhelms the poetry". And about his creative imagery, "Webb is a poet of awesome inquiry. It is through the richness of his metaphor-making that Webb places an original strain on the language such that he creates a world of rich inquiry". James Tulip, Australian poetry critic, wrote that 'reading Francis Webb is like wrestling with an angel'. No one would disagree that wrestling is involved: just decoding the syntax can be a challenge in many of these poems, then there are compacted metaphors, elusive rhyme schemes, buried religious references, and an expectation that the reader will be as alarmingly erudite as the poet.

1.4 Schizophrenic Language

As we have already seen, little is knows about the nature of schizophrenia: it can only be regarded as a reaction specific to a state

---

[18] Thanks to the Toby Davidson for kindly making me available an electronic version of his Collected Poems, which has been used to evaluate various quantitative aspects of Francis Webb's poetic work.

of anxiety originated in the infancy of the sufferer from this disease, which is newly experienced later in life. In this early stage, the reaction of the mentally ill to his society is an escape from all contacts with his terrifying and threatening surroundings. The turning away of the patient from the external world, shows up as a state of morbid introversion where he can live his delusion undisturbedly.

The sufferers from the mental disease called schizophrenia are locked up in mental hospitals which too often are institutions for putting away individuals who could not maintain their place in society. There, their condition usually worsens: after being treated they should be brought into renewed contact with the world around them, from which they have cut themselves off. But more often, they are only well cared for materially and allowed to pine away mentally in their isolation. Usually – and that is referred to the past and first half of last 20th century – they underwent treatment with E.C.T., which is no longer regarded by most psychiatrists as a convenient and adequate therapy, but was at least until the 1970s.

On the contrary, according to most parties nowadays, it increases mental disturbance and leads to a slow regression. In an advanced stage, the sufferer from schizophrenia is unable to resume his work as well as a decent place in society: there is a marked retardation in thought and actions, which can progress to the extent that one can speak of a stupor in which the patient becomes completely inactive.

The flight from life, the inability to enter into emotional contacts with the external world turns into a tendency to interiorization, to imaginative construction and symbolism. A psychopathologic theory sees in schizophrenic language[19] and thought a regression to patterns belonging to primitive, archaic thought. Words are endowed with a

---

[19] For many of my comments and ideas in this section I relied on Sergio Pirro, 1967. Il linguaggio schizofrenico, Milano, 1st ed.

magic power. Thought is characterized by a regression to prelogical thinking. These studies equate thought and speech processes of the schizophrenic subject with those of primitives and of children. In the thought of prelogical kind, the effect produced by images in the observer is believed to be an inherent quality of the object, which thus acquires magic power. The paralogician accepts the identity based upon identical predicates.

But the presence of mythic, ritual, magic elements in schizophrenic thought could also be regarded as a discovery and re-evaluation of the irrational element existing in man, that civilization cannot do away with. A scientific approach to schizophrenic language and thought takes into account the experimental data derived from direct observation, and does not try to build theories external to it, to be superimposed upon it. In this sense, schizophrenic language is the language used by a certain group of people called schizophrenics by psychiatrists, on the basis of diagnosed evaluations; it could also be defined as the amount of linguistic disturbances derived from the study of schizophrenic subjects.

Natural language is a system of signs endowed with referential meaning established by custom and mutual assent; this system of signs can be communicated intentionally from a sender to a received who is willing to interpret it. Signs differ from signals, which are events indicating other events in an univocal way; they indicate the past, present or future existence of a certain condition or event and are coupled with it in a unique way. Whereas signs are not linked to the event by an immediate, direct relationship. They have a double relation: with the object and with the interpreter; in this sense, they are largely autonomous.

Natural language is made up of a plurality of signs; poetry carries emotional meaning with its referential meaning, and sometimes is highly symbolic. Symbols belong to complex symbolizing structures with a high degree of abstraction, linked with metaphor and metonymy-based speech building processes. Language externalizes personal experience, makes it possible to refer to something that is not present but only remembered; it can be studied as behaviour. The main function of language is that of putting us in contact with other people, that is it enables us to communicate. If we speak of semantics of schizophrenic language we look for a meaning in the words of schizophrenics. Semantics and psychology go together in this case: we cannot split intentionality from achievement of meaning. To speak about meaning is to speak about the whole dimension of a patient language behaviour.

Meaning is regarded as a vast infrastructure made up of cognitive and emotional relationships: something means something because it is immediately fitted into the totality of the psychic flux where it is inextricably bound. The emergence of meaning is the result of highly complex mental processes occurring in the entire psychic structure of the subject, it is linked to the whole of his being. The psyche, in its total structure reacts to the presence of a new element or item by including it, as in a mosaic, in a continuum of relations; its features interact with analogous features of preexisting items into a whole, where it is defined in relation to other semantic fields and then interpreted,

The building of an acceptable and meaningful sentence entails a remarkable widening of the semantic network as a result of the interrelations between its components. This amplifying process does not result in an uncontrolled or incoherent new unit, which includes cahotic or unselected series of relations; useless or non complementary linkages are excluded or deleted automatically from the meaningful series. The new semantic unit emerges not only from a synthesis of all semantic fields but also from a filtering off of all incompatible elements. If this filter is lacking, we are in presence of schizophrenic language. This condition, which can be defined as semantic dissociation, is basically a tendency to very unusual generalizations and over-inclusions: ideas become included in concepts distantly related to other ideas.

But generalization is a different thing from over-inclusion: whereas the former is the use of signs on a higher abstract level, the latter is the non-deletion of marginal elements beyond the usual and customary semantic halo of an idea, so that the concept becomes disturbed and distorted. In his isolation, the schizophrenic subject breaks into pieces the semantic network necessary to communicate with other people and produces highly ambiguous speech.

There are various levels of semantic dissociation: in its early stage, it is basically a widening out of the referential structure, a loosening of the nexus connecting signs to the semantic referential and emotional infrastructure indispensable to build meaning. Thus, the pragmatic meaning of signs fades out, and the area of semantic fluctuation becomes wider and wider. There is a disturbing atmosphere in which every sign is endowed with multiple roles; the displacement of meaning leads to newly-formed and distorted signs, where we have a slipping of meaning from one word to another. The result is a decrease of the significance of the whole. Contaminations, overlappings, and interferences of meaning appear, until a complete emptying out of the sign pattern occurs and we are left with uncoordinated and incoherent motor-behaviour.

As the disease progresses, sentences become formally disorganized, their grammatical and syntactic structure undergoes serious alterations, until it goes entirely lost. Hence, in its early stage, semantic dissociation prefigures itself as the achievement of a formal freedom, as a release from conventional patterns of language behaviour. But to free oneself from a network of limiting references opens the way to an expressiveness no longer bound to conventional and traditional channels of communication, and it freely opens itself to more personal and original ways of creative expression. It contributes to enhance the emotional echoes and halos, as well as suggestiveness of the discourse. This stage, which could have been experienced by Webb, can be regarded as a highly positive phase of creative writing.

On the contrary, in an advanced stage of the disease, language is no longer used by the schizophrenic in order to communicate or express something: it is rather the object of playful and automatic manipulation. In the early stage, the schizophrenic seems particularly keen to an excessive use of generalized signs, vague expressions, useless or pleonastic adjectivations; it is very common the use of metaphors, metonymies, and symbolic expressions which fit particularly well into his abstracting tendency. In the later stage, there is a tendency to create new words or to use a word instead of another more appropriate word, which is then enriched by a new grammar and syntax. The style becomes very peculiar: it is filled up with grotesque, deformed, eccentric and incomprehensible expressions, until there is a complete gap between sign and meaning.

Schizophrenic language becomes partly or totally verbal game, playing with vowels, sounds, bits of words; discourse is characterized by short sentences without complex syntax; sentences are linked by assonance, consonance, alliterations; meaning disappears, a complete semantic dissolution takes place. There is a deletion of certain categories of words, like for instance, articles, personal pronouns, demonstrative pronouns, conjunctions, adverbs and other function words; it is very common the use of the infinitive. The leaving out of these function words or sentence formers results in a sort of telegraphic style, or "word salad": discourse becomes a mere sequence of significant words, without links – semantic or syntactic – whatsoever;

the order of words in the sentence is frequently inverted, it is upside down; syntactic ellipsis is also used.

Webb might as well have undergone this process of mental decay; but the deterioration of his language behaviour could hardly be detected in his poetic work, as we shall see further on. The only thing we can affirm is that, at a certain point of his life after 1964, Webb reduced his poetry writing activity. Perhaps this was the sign that his mental disease was progressing beyond the point of no return.

In fact Webb did more than simply create rhetoric poetic devices suitable for his poems, he used a process that may be defined as "transposition". If we look at the definition or meaning of the word "transposition": we see that it may refer to a process of "transferring from one place or period to another" that is spatiotemporal dislocation; or else it can be referred to music and in this case it means to "put a piece of music from one key into another (to be played by a different instrument)". In fact, this is what happens with a poem, when the reader is ideally transferred in an abstract spatiotemporal dimension, by using the words in another "key".

Now this is the essence and the magics of Francis Webb's poetry and in this he is a master, perhaps the greatest or certainly one of the greatest poets, because his style is mainly featuring this technique. Of course we know that poetry uses words in a special way, differently from prose writing, by means of a wealth of rhetorical devices that are directed to divert the reader from assigning to words their common meaning. I will comment this point at length below with plenty of examples taken from his poetic work. Here I just want to emphasize the point expressed in the title and reported above: Webb's poetry is characterized by a laborious and highly specialized technique that, starting from usual rhetorical and rhythmic devices – like the use of metaphors and similes, and a richness in assonances, alliterations and rhymes – converges from a certain moment onward to recreate in the poem sensations and feelings directly from the poetic texture and this is done "by an introjection of point of view".

The reader is thus taken from an objective point of view – the one guided by the poet - into a subjective internal and "immanent" perspective that serves the same aim, but in a much deeper manner[20]. There are usually two ways for making metaphors[21]: one patent, explicit and another hidden, implicit that I clarify below. But then Webb has invented a new way to produce metaphors which is what I define "immanent": and this is partly done by intention to induce a change of perspective, a transposition in the level and type of metaphoric awareness.

The normal, explicit or extended way is the one that is achieved by means of external grammatical or linguistic links – conjunctions "like" and "as", simple coordinating or disjoining conjunctions - between members of a metaphor, simile, analogy, or any other figure of speech; the other way is achieved by the deletion or erasure of these external, explicit linguistic elements, and as a result the two or more members of the metaphor are now adjacent, juxtaposed. It's partly the result of a stylistic change from an explicit (to the reader) use of rhetorical devices into an asyndetic style where synaesthesia is the rule. And the words play a different role from the norm, realizing completely the sense of "estrangement", defamiliarization or "Ostranene" as Viktor Schlovsky (or Shklovsky, Sklovskij) defined it[22], which is typical of true work of art. But as I said, this is one side of coin: what really makes the

---

[20] See also Ashcroft, 1974
[21] See Shutova et al., 2013
[22] In studying poetic speech in its phonetic and lexical structure as well as in its characteristic distribution of words and in the characteristic thought structures compounded from the words, we find everywhere the artistic trademark – that is, we find material obviously created to remove the automatism of perception; the author's purpose is to create the vision which results from that deautomatized perception. A work is created "artistically" so that its perception is impeded and the greatest possible effect is produced through the slowness of the perception. (Shklovsky, 1970: 19)

difference is the new perspective or internal point of view offered to the reader. I will delve deeply into this topic in a section below.

As Chris Wallace Crabbe comments in his book[23] words have a double function:

> "This loved medium, then, may be used as message, as expressive stuff or as sheer play-dough. Such verse as we take seriously will incorporate both communication and expression."(ibid.,3)

In particular, then, after having equated poetry with painting and declaring that all that really matters are "images", he comments:

> "The essence of post-romantic poetry is the endeavour to bring it up rich. Like van Gogh, or Cezanne, or the cubists, they are working their medium so that the whole surface is active, vivacious, animating. Webb, Hart Crane, Lowell, Murray, these are potent examples." (ibid.4)

where Webb comes first in the list of poets. I am not here referring to abstract and religious notions of meaning which were certainly also part of Webb's main inspiration. What I really want to tackle is the question of characterizing meaning from a linguistic point of view. Further on in his essay Chris W.Crabbe reaches the core the heart of the main theme related to poetic language, where he writes:

> Wisdom poetry is metamorphic. The task of its language is to transform the grainy facts of temporal discourse into gems whose facets are capable of reflecting a glimpse of some eternal truth. Under this aspect, the aims of poetry can be seen to be paradoxical. It employs and energizes verbal structures in

---

[23] Chris Wallace Crabbe, p.3-4.

order to create a temporary home for that which is by definition not a part of language: that is to say, for the mystical.

1.5 Allegories and Symbols

Symbols are a direct product of the power of abstraction, which is given to man when he begins to realize that there is an outer world from which he can detach himself: this is when he learns how to master and to possess it through its representation in symbols, metaphors, images charged with more or less implicit meaning, that is to say through words and the language. Ontogenetically and phylogenetically speaking, this process takes place in an advanced phase of man's development. Children and primitives are not able to produce symbols; whenever they produce images these are not meant to "represent" a thing, they "are" a thing.

When man begins to detach himself from the outer world and to develop the analytical and scientific attitude to things, he starts to use independent carriers to hold his meanings. But the counterpart to the symbol-making activity of the human mind is, as I said, its power of apprehending and mastering reality. This is partly due to the poem liar quality of the symbol of compressing and concentrating a whole range of meanings from reality into one single image – which can be a word, a sound, a gesture, an object, etc. The symbol has then two opposite and interfused functions: it detaches and reconciles the subject and the object.

In what way does a symbol differ from an allegory? The fundamental function of the symbol is that of enhancing our grip on reality; allegory, on the contrary, has the function of abstracting from reality, of emptying the object from its meaning in order to impose a highly subjective and incongruous meaning: as Frederic Jameson says, "...allegory is precisely the dominant mode of expression of a world in which things have been for whatever reason utterly sundered from meaning, from spirit, from genuine human existence"[24]. Further on he quotes from Benjamin:

> "Allegories are in the realm of thoughts that ruins are in the realm of things... Once the object has... become allegorical, once life has flowed out of it, the object itself remains behind, dead, yet preserved for all eternity; it lies before the allegorist, given over to him utterly, for good or ill. In other words, the object itself is henceforth incapable of projecting any meaning on its own; it can only take on that meaning which the allegorist wishes to lend it. He instills it with his own meaning, himself descends to inhabit it: and this must be understood not psychologically but in an ontological sense. In his hands the thing in question becomes something else, speaks of something else, becomes for him the key to some realm of hidden knowledge, as whose emblem he honors it."[ibid. p.71-2]

This leads us back to the distinction between the religious symbolical and the allegorical poet: the symbol-maker is thus set in clear perspective to the allegorist. Both poets draw the material for their symbols and images from the realm of religion and mythology. But while is the former a poem's symbols are the spontaneous product of an unconscious mental process, where the genuinely creative artist expresses feelings, emotions, and perceptions, in the latter images are evoked by a highly cerebral mental mechanism. In this sense the religious symbolical poet is close to the primitive and the child in the first phase of the creative process: his mythopoiesis is a "belief" in the

---

[24] Frederic Jameson, 1971. Marxism and Form: Twentieth-Century Dialectical Theories of Literature, Princeton, New Jersey, p.71

reality of the object, because he transfuses into the poem part of his being; it is not merely an autonomous representation of well-wrought images.

Poets draw the material for their symbols from the realm of religion and mythology not so much because the most striking images are to be found in those fields, but rather because it is only those realms that provide the symbols that can affect directly the reader's imagination. With the religious symbolical poet, myths and symbols do not become a substitute for reality; they call for empathy, oneness with the object, they realize an identity, an ontological tangency by which elements empirically distinct blend into the one pattern of the poem. In this way, symbols and myths are not just a device; they become rather the only suitable vehicle to convey the authenticity of a given experience.

The opposition between symbolic and allegorical poetry is hinged on the concept of dualism. The allegorical poet uses religious and mythological material in such a way as to (and more often in order to) affirm and establish the primacy of subject upon object, spirit upon matter, supernatural upon natural, conscious upon unconscious. This dualistic view of the world is a result or a basically romantic and idealistic position[25].

According to idealism, man is the subjective ego that lends reality to the exterior world of natural and social phenomena; in other words, the subject is inflated at the expense of the object, the exterior world. In this context, allegory is intended as the effacement of the object in favour of the emergency of a new entity of an abstract nature. In line with this position, the allegorical poet superimposes upon his material an external and highly subjective view, which intentionally modifies

---

[25] See J.Hillis Miller, 1966. Poets of Reality – Six Twentieth-Century Writers, Cambridge Mass.

and distorts the primal content and meaning of myth. The poem will, then, appear to be lacking in internal harmony, or will reveal the existence of a dichotomy either between the material used and the treatment of the poet, or between language and content.

More often, however, the clash is revealed in the attempt to match the use of traditional images with a contemporary context. In either case, the presence of an internal clash or dichotomy is the symptom of the poet's escapism, of an idealistic attitude towards his inner and outer reality. As a result of dualistic thinking, the poet will end up by marring the creative potentialities of his work.

The religious and symbolic mode stems basically from the reconciling function of myth, when properly used. Mythical thinking is manifested in artistic activity whenever the artist's concern is not hindered by subjectivism and dualistic thought. Mythical thinking erases the duality of subject and object and creates relationships; it is analogical in kind, and it operates through the opposition and consequent combination of irreconcilable terms such as life and death, change and permanence, peace and war, nature and culture. It acknowledges the dualism inherent in the world of man but, unlike dualistic thought, it does not strive for the prevalence of one set of values at the expense of the other. Rather it conceives of man, society and history as a system of relationships in which everything is relative, and related to everything else.

Likewise, the poet strives for a poetry in which he can express a unity of feeling, a mythical view of the world which is not opposed to the historical; it takes into account the opposites and encompasses them in the relatively enclosed world of the poem. His poetry is symbolic and not allegorical: it concentrates meanings rather than hiding them; the religious and mythological material is introduced as harmonically grafted on to his personality, his historical current social and existential condition, rather than imposed upon it.

1.6 Using the WORD, WORDS and MEANING

Now, words and meaning were always an important theme in Webb's poetry and part of his imagery. So I will start my exploration of Webb's Collected Poems [26] by looking into a number of themes starting from the use of "word/words" and "meaning". This can be revelatory of Webb's internal attitude and feeling. Then I will look into other important components of his poetic imagery. As will become clear from the excerpts reported below, Webb uses "word/words/meaning" very sparingly and with an alternating but overall mostly negative general feeling: words are the ingredients of poetry but choosing the right words is a struggle which may be painful.

The poet is depicted as a "word-haunted" man in *On First Hearing a Cuckoo*. But then "word" is then equated with "World" thus acquiring an all-embracing value. We find the first use in *A Tip For Saturday*,

> The navigator's task affords
> Small safety from a spate of words.

where "words" seem to play a positive role. In *Images in Winter* "word" is a member of a strong metaphor, where it becomes "stray" and is compared to a "stoned" bird, no longer a positive image: "A stray word fell like a stoned bird from the lips."

In *From Leichhardt Pantomime* "words" fall again "glibly" from "motionless" lips, again non positive image, "Words fall glibly enough from motionless lips", or further on in the same poem

---

[26] In this chapter and in the following I will always be referring to Toby Davidson's new edition already cited

> Which is pertinent:
> Our Prince towering through anguish to purpose, or our Prince
> Bombarding blockhead stars with curious words?

where "words" become "curious" and are the object of a rhetoric question in which they are hypothetically bombarding "blockhead" stars. A conflicting image is the one associated to "words" in *Author's Prologue*

> nor will her love
> Flicker and throb from the smoulder of fine words.

words are "fine" but are the object of "smoulder". Again specifically indicated as negative feeling in *A Whaler*, "They give you a smile and words like knives when behind you": here words have become like "knives". In Two on the Map it seems that "words" have recovered positive value:

> You may write words or ride in omnibuses,
> Give lectures, name a river, kill a man,

It is in the poems dedicated to Leichhardt expedition that we find the most inspired uses of "words" in his poetry. In *The First Expedition* "words" are again the first part of a metaphor which has positive import,

> But loose rock's singing on the cliff–face, flurry of words
> Parting the dried lips of a watercourse?

However when we look at *The Second Expedition* we find again a negative flavour,

> A vapid trickle of fever
> Seeps into the men: they brandish at each other
> Dulled edges of words.

Eventually, in *The Third Expedition*, "words" become equated with "world", and in fact for the poet the world is in the words he uses in his poems,

> Cross to the field pitched beyond world and words.
> ...
> yield to the pressure
> And silence of their fate. World, words, are closer.

more specifically in the following stanzas we find the most revealing verse

> It is where sun and world blossom into words
> As a tree's lovely frenzies of bloom divide
> Winter from winter, month from month of birds:

The world "blossoms" into words: this is certainly true of Webb's poetry where his craftsmanship is always focussed on the search of the right words to forge and mould his metaphors. Further on in *Serenade to the Favourite Movie-Actress*, words are "dead"; in *Melville at Woods Hole* words are "like firebreaks", again a positive value.

Words become "antiphonal" in *The Telescopes* and then they are the transposition of the cuckoo's typical call, "two words" in *On first hearing a cuckoo*. Two "unchanging" words, always the "same two words". But then towards the end of the poem, words recover their negative import,

> Not spring, not Surrey, no, nor merely
> A dead word–haunted man. Two words remained—
> The language foreign, childish perhaps, or pitiable—

The poet is a "word-haunted" man. In *The Gunner* words are "those of the dream" and are spoken by the world, again the union of these two images to deliver a concept of wholeness: words are as the world a unity of all possible senses. Finally in *Harry* words are unspeakable,

> Comes the day when his mother realizes all.
> Few questions, and a chaos of silence. Her thin eyes
> Are emptied. Doors rattle in the house,
> Foundations stagger. The Beginning becomes us;
> And he is mulcted of words, remain to him only
> The words of sin, escape, which is becoming all of life.

On the contrary, the word "meaning" is used only few times and mainly with a negative import, and sometimes in the form of the adjective "meaningless". Only in one of his early poems, the word "meaning" is used in a positive literal way, the poem is *An Old Record*, and the citation is this:

> This jaded earth props and staggers - give me meaning
> For spur, or a call from the garbled scrub of the night;

Until at the very end of his production, the word becomes capitalized, "Meaning" thus transformed into a religious symbol. We find it clearly in *Light*,

> Time labours towards a meaning upon the wrist
> —Never His meaning; can He be risen?

Then in *Self-portrait* as a predication of the subject "creation",

> An outline of fullness soberly embraced
> By shadow of widest meaning is creation.

and in *Before Two Girls*,

> They forsook the amorous dust for immaculate Meaning,

Only to find that same dust

The book is organized into six chapters: Chapter II, "The Alienated Identity", focuses mainly on the progression in Webb's poetry of his feelings of separateness from society. The language will reveal the presence in the imagery of pairs of opposites: in this phase Webb tends to situate his self between these opposites in the attempt to create a midway world, a balanced dimension for his psyche in search of harmony, order and peace. The myth of Christ is referred to only fragmentarily in the poems belonging to this phase.

Chapter III, "Towards the Creation of a Personal Myth", and Chapter IV, "The Struggle for Survival", are more comprehensive and span Webb's career from maturity to the end of his poetic activity. The titles draw attention to the transformation of his creative genius from a mythico-religious into a mythic phenomenon, as a result of his complete endorsement of the myth of Christ. In this way his poetic word starts to reach beyond the boundaries of allegories. In other words, Chapter III and IV are concerned with the development of Webb's personal myth of the alienated and suffering artist, mentally ill and as such rejected on a physical level by his society. To this end he moulds his poetry on the basis of the Christian tradition – being raised as a Catholic – as an extrapolation that satisfies his spiritual and moral feelings. In particular, in Chapter II his creation is motivated by his need to justify and accept his existential condition and his social role; in Chapter III the myth becomes a shelter from the evils of society. It is in this last phase that we assist at a gradual deterioration of his poetic themes and language, until his entire silence.

Chapter V and VI offer a computational and a quantitative approach to the corpus of Webb's poetry with the intention to highlight its intrinsic uniqueness.

CHAPTER II: THE ALIENATED IDENTITY

2.1 The early poems

The early poems are very revealing as to a proper understanding of Webb's later poetry, since they show fully his preoccupation with the identity problem. He is painfully aware of his role as the existential wanderer – of vague romantic origins – in search of truth. He is also very concerned with his role inside society. In "Palace of Dreams" (p.24) the poet's consciousness, the "I", is set in contrast to the deep black haunting and "oblivious" night. On the one side we have the poet's consciousness and on the other side the unconscious: the poet itself is s prefiguration of the voyage of the eternal and romantic wanderer into the realm of inspiration and creativity. It is a realm of pain and suffering, where sleep and oblivion are regarded as "the only key" to the poet's soul. And the contents of his unconscious, the purveyor of his secret knowledge, are "Hieroglyphed with secret sign", in scrolls to be deciphered in "loneliness". The contact with the dark realm of the unconscious is depicted here, as in his later poetry, as an excruciating and tormenting experience: the "I", which closes in the first and last stanza, is opposed to such compounds as "deep-grained", "solid-hewn", and to adnominations such as "moon-starts", "death-dewed".

Another rendering of the same theme is given in "Night Swimming"(p.28), where the poet enlarges the field of connotations. Night is associated with water, a recurrent image for the unconscious in dreams. The associations in the poem convey an impression of pain, of anguish, of fear and violence. The poem's last word is "death" and the central images deal with was: we are presented again with the struggle of the "I", the conscious ego, with the unconscious, a struggle which is rendered in the last stanza with the metaphor "the strong fire writhing in its wooden fetters". The unconscious is given its connotations by a series of metaphors which span from the naturalistic to the expressionistic: the "silver water shimmering" is "Waiting to cradle you in a sudden, cool embrace". The threat of being swallowed by it is reinforced by the metaphor "black throat of night". The connotation of the word "ripple", which is associated with "grace" in the first stanza, is extended in the third stanza where the word is set in a different context, recalling its secondary meaning – that of a toothed implement that removes seeds from plants. Thus the image of the "ripple" is turned into a blister made by a whip, the which of the sea of the unconscious where the "whipped sprays" crumble "like columns crashing"; waves are thus transformed into a ridge, a weal on the skin of the sea. Violence is expressed also by bodies that "knife the clear moonlight", while their arms gleam "like swords".

In "To a Poet"(p.29) Webb examines his role inside society: his concern is mainly with the sterility of poetic imagination in our "gangrened world", which in "Compliments to the Audience"(p.34), a poem dealing with the same theme, is reiterated as "gangrened cities". The role of the poet is also examined in a series of poems where Webb presents us with a recurrent image in his work: that of the fool. It appears in "Night Swimming"(p.28) as the "motley", and it will appear in a later poem of this phase, "Middle Harbour"(p.38). In "Cap and Bells"(p.30), the poet-fool is the central theme; here Webb refurbishes the imagery of the previous poems and the same elements of violence are represented with more cogency. "Tonight the stars are yellow sparks/Dashed out from the moon's hot steel"; "darkness" is "crannied by lights"; and "each naked light trails a sabre/Of blue steel".

The piercing of consciousness through the darkness of the unconscious entails pain and suffering, says the poet; even the sea-voyage on the dark waters of the unconscious is given negative annotations. The poet has reached the "harbour", where he is surrounded by "grave great peace". The combined effect of the assonance and the alliteration enhances the semantic import of the epithet "grave" and draws attention to its meaning as a noun: the harbour is thus equated to a tomb. The return to the harbour is viewed both as a positive and as a negative event: the harbour is safe because it is balanced between earth and water, consciousness and the unconscious. But this safety is not disjoined from the poet's awareness of having gone through and beyond anguish and despair, and having attained the "grave great peace". Webb's realization of his role as poet-fool is here intimately linked to his existential condition; the realization of his tragic role as the outcast, the wanderer of "Palace of Dreams" is, then, associated with the amount of pain involved in the creative process, conceived as externalization of unconscious contents of the psyche. The same awareness is expressed in "Compliments to the Audience"(p.34):

"...we are ready, so many gaping wounds
For the crude application of salt, or a malted morphine.

And further on,

How's this: we are giant things trapped in an endless mural,
Sad rebels oiled into timeless agony,
Fixed by the artist Fate to gestures of peril?
We dress up in silent suffering and dignity" (p.6)

The same violence involved in the creative process is present in "The Mountains"(p.43), where the poet in his creative moment is "Stumbling through channels of silence", and has "to twist along/Paths of the wounded light". In "Images in Winter"(p.36) Webb introduces for the first time the myth of Christ in the lines:

"That tattered swagman, Death on a Friday night
May pop in with the appropriate metaphor,"

where he not only emphasizes the extraordinariness of the event by inserting capital letters, but also differentiates it from the rest of the poem with a technical device, which he will repeat in "Middle Harbour": he abstracts the line from the rhyme-scheme with a different ending word, in this case "night". At the same time, the metaphor in the first of these lines is referred to in the second as a metaphor on how to make metaphors: it becomes a sort of meta-metaphor.

The reference to Christ as "the appropriate metaphor" will be resumed in most of his later poetry as a means to extrapolate his belief in the need to revivify and resurrect, as it were, worn-out images through the appropriate metaphoric association. The task of the poet resurrector-of-images is envisaged in "Images in Winter" in the necessity to recapture the momentariness of vision and to transform it into metaphors.

"Middle Harbour"(p.38) is the most representative poem of this phase: its central image, the harbour standing in the middle and mediating between two poles, sea and earth, dark and light, symbolizes the condition of the poet divided between consciousness and the unconscious. The poem is built on the dialectical interplay of these two poles, while expressing the momentariness of an equilibrium, of a visionary balance.

The opposing forces are concentrated and intertwined in the first stanza: in the chiastic construction of the first two lines where "depth" and "height" look for a balance; "dimness" and "light" are "wedded" in the fourth line; and in the last two lines

"...the curving brilliance leaps

And shivers back to the dark lungs of the water".

In fact, Webb could not find a better receptacle for his opposites than water and the sea, where all forms of life on earth sprang from the cosmic chaos.[27] In the second stanza Webb supplies us with a further example of his poetic skill: the fourth line is a reiteration of his recurrent metaphor,

"Perfect impact of peace, and one fool apart"

which is perfectly integrated into the structure of the stanza, both syntactically and rhythmically. Its cogency is determined by the scansion of this verse as to the total rhyme scheme, which parallels it to the last line of the stanza. This line has been isolated from the rhyme in order to introduce the myth of Christ:

"You have been well paid: take up your purse and go?"

which seems to refer to Judas, the traitor of Christ. The parallelism between the fourth and the last line of the stanza is reinforced by the rhyme of the preceding lines: "eye" rhymes only with "cry". The final stanza ends with a further reference to the "motley", the fool's particoloured dress, which appeared previously in "Night Swimming". The motley stands also as a synthesis of opposite and clashing elements, as they have been related in the first stanza. Webb gives urgency to the ending lines by reducing the syntactical nexus, by using an infinitive, and by relating the three clauses by means of a parataxis.

Besides the fool's dress was indirectly referred to as "Jacob's coat of a few jaded colours" in the second line of the last stanza, that the poet "will cast down" because it might become "a shadow of discord", as it did in the story narrated in the Bible where the coat given by his father

---

[27] It is worth reminding that he passed most of his life as child and a boy with his grand-father, who died when he was 12, and who transmitted his great passion for sailing and the sea to Frank.

caused Jacob's brothers jealousy and ended up with the brothers selling him as a slave.

With "An Old Record"(p.39) Webb adds to his imagery another layer of correspondences both on a semantic and on a symbolic level with the opposition between illusion and reality: the "stage-convention" of the second line, which may be connected to the metaphor of the poet as an actor on the stage of life, introduced already in "Compliments to the Audience". This additional layer in the total sum of the imagery works out in terms of "candle" and "shadow", light and dark, and is meant to add a note of uncertainly to reality. In the simile "as in our vague dreams", Webb seems to affirm once more the interchangeability of dreams, fantasy, illusion and reality, as well as the inconsistency and the instability of the premises on which is based the poet's private world, his being-in-the-world. The time dimension, symbolized by the recurrent image of the "inquiring clock", sets in as a disruptive element, "allotting its due of panic to each day", and brings in the thought of death, which is equalled to a "shock", whereas life is depicted as a "lapse". Webb's irony, a consequence of his *Weltanschaung*, is always lurking in the background, and notably here by a clause in a stylized language, "as I might say".

Nautical or marine imagery, [again taken from direct experience with his grand-father] which has already been widely exploited in "Cap and Bells" and in "Images in Winter", is predominant in this poem: the "derelict thought" associated with "event" by an asyndeton, is turned respectively into "spent hulls, reefs of the future, and danger". The "hull", another recurrent image in Webb's work, is used here as objective correlative: the "old record" becomes the hull, to testify to past events, memories, illusions and realities which become interchangeable in the process of creation and recreation of the reader's mind. The first stanza includes such words as "tack", "slack", "drift", "pirate", "port" all derived from nautical language.

The following stanzas develop the same language, but not as a mere transcription, or as a transliteration from one language into another: the metaphysical dimension is a transfiguration through metaphors, in order to renew the life of words, Webb's basic aim throughout his work:

> "For properties – I am the shadow and glimmer;
> My clean-poised thought like an otter will strike after
> Some warped glint in the depths, a silver tremor,
> Still careless if all it finds be a stone in the water.
> In this powdering light on the shaken yellow beach
> I finger a salvaged-shred, bleached waxen shell
> Still shivering with fugitive passion of a bell
> Epic of drama and storm passed out reach –
> Yet death, hungry for fragments, switches back a long
> Tentacle from that storm: the bell swept out so far
> Is quarry for the throttling wind; so your fading song
> Swings out in cadence like a falling star."

Life and death, illusion and reality are transfused in the images of the hull, the shell, the bell, which are charged with profound meaning. The poet himself, in his recollection of the shipwreck, and in his creative process are part of the same universe of life and death, of creation and recreation. Then, on this borderline world – the beach of the harbour – he asks of the night, the personification of his unconscious:

> "... give me meaning
> For spur, or a call from the garbled scrub of the night."

The poet, like Roland, is ready to risk martyrdom for his faith: if

Roland refused to blow the horn in order to call for help against the pagans, he seems ready – even if with an ironical self-awareness of the perils implied by his act – to make pacts with the underworld, his unconscious.

In "Bridgehead"(p.41) Webb presents us again with the usual scenery of beach and sea, but this time the spatial dimension is pushed to its physical limits: the bridgehead, the frontier where one accedes to the enemy's territory, represents all that belongs to the "otherness" in ourselves. Significantly enough, the bridgehead has been situated on the borderline that has left a "chain of footprints" on the sand, was heading from the sea, the perilous realm of the unconscious. Light has been given again a painful connotation: "lightning laid weals on the rigid arch of the sky". The intruder coming from the unconscious into consciousness has brought pain and "despair". In the third stanza, the poem acquires a wider cosmic dimension and a more realistic tone: planets are stirred up by the "spattering gullies of the thunder", where "spatter" conveys the sound of pellets.

Webb has gathered all forces of creation, the earth, the sea, the rain, lightning and thunder, and the planets to witness to a cosmic war: images and sound coalesce in a dramatic sequence where man's self is crashed down to leave room to Webb's anthropomorphic representations of nature. Death is personified with "frozen flanks", the rain has "crooked hands", thunder becomes "the lifted muzzle/Of laughter wedging into the snarling skies"; while man's eyes "Grope back for the smile of the sun".

The disembodiment of the human presences in favour of an animistic view of natural forces, with their negative interference, contributes to create an inversion of values in the world of man, so that:

"That quaking light played zigzag tricks around
Our starting bridges of sight and sanity;

The thunderstorm has not only subverted the order of natural processes; through its metaphorical relation to war, it has also overturned the system of values in the world of man. The poem ends with a metaphor which combines different semantic field, "the ironic laughter of sunrise", working as an anticlima in the haunting rhythm of the poem.

2.2 First Appearance of Mental Illness

After 1947, Webb's life was going to change because of the first appearance of his "mental illness". About this time, he published "*Leichhardt in Theatre*", which was to be transformed after his return from England in 1950, and was finally published in 1952. In 1943 he volunteered for the R.A.A.F. and went to Canada, where he served for 18 months. Much of this time he was doing flying training, which he completed and became flight sergeant. But at that time, in 1945, the war ended and he was demobilized, whilst still in Canada at the flying school. So he returned to Australia. In fact, Webb never did fly on his own, nor took part in a mission: one could say that Canada represented his frustrated expectations, which in fact were partly realized by his activity as athlete, running the mile. He regarded himself a distance runner slightly above average[28].

When he returned, after having published "*A Drum for Ben Boyd*" in 1946, he had already realized that he was unable to stay at the university, like all "normal" people, and that he was an exceptionally sensitive human being. Thus, on the one side he was unable to behave

---

[28] from a letter reported in God's Fool by Michael Griffith, p. 89

as a "normal" person, on the other he was affirming his difference, his deviance from he norm: in both cases, his illness was starting to assume a definite physiognomy. When he went to England, he has his first "breakdown". On his return to Australia in 1950, he did all kinds of jobs, including that of jackeroo. During the period from 1950 to 1952 he must have undergone profound psychological and spiritual crises which bear upon the course of his future life, both as a man and as a poet.

The poems of this period are all characterized by a regression into the unconscious: most of them tell of travels on sea or land for the discovery of Australia. But Webb is concerned with the rationale informing these poems, and in particular with the symbolic meaning of death by water. In fact these poems tell either of shipwrecks, or, in the case of Leichhardt's death, of man's failure after having attempted too much. In "Advertisement"(p.104) Sturt's death is turned from a death in the desert sands, into a death in the last stanza of the sequence. Thus, if it is true that the sea is the homeland of the traveller-explorer, or of the romantic wanderer in search of his self, it is also clear that every attempt to overcome the mystery and power of the sea-unconscious in this phase is meant to turn into a tragic failure.

The process of piercing from consciousness into the unconscious is still felt as a painful one: Webb is struggling for the acceptance of his unconscious, a struggle which, in Jungian terms, is related to the *Shadow*, the dark side of man's psyche. His concern with the image of light is paramount in this phase: we found it already in the early poems; it is present in the poems belonging to *A Drum for Ben Boyd*, where light "quakes"(p.83), "contracts", and "drives on". Further on we find "churned up"(p.83) light, "snippets of lightning", "crazy and wandering light"; and then using our star, the sun, we get "our blazing barracks of the sun"(p.84), "an immense shaking of the sun"(p.85). Only at the end of the sequence is light associated with shadow: Ben Boyd is depicted as

"a shadow at the distant end
Of a tunnel of sunlight"(p.102).

In the poem "The Hulks of Noumea"(p.45), a poem written in this period, there is a rather gloomy metaphor dealing obliquely with light:

"The dry, yellow throat of dawn is eager to drain
Draughts of legend and kindness that night spills"

where the accumulation of alliterative sounds in "dry", "dawn", "draughts" contributes an effect of painful awareness. The same applies to the poems belonging to the other sequence, *Leichhardt Pantomime*: in "Introduction in a Wax-works"(p.69), the metaphor "a freezing douche of light" is counterpoised by "all this shadow-craze"; while in "Advertisement"(p.104) where Webb deals with Sturt's expedition, we find

"Light has rapped at his skull, flooded into his heart,
Shrivelled, consumed him. Light has tracked and curled
  Its searing wake over touch and vision and retreat."

and further on,

"... He will lie again
Racked by light and the heat..."

The fragment "Disaster Bay"(p.48) contains two metaphors indirectly related to light, the first one deals with the night,

"... No one may trust the night
That plucks response from things lodged deep in the mind,
Omens, unreason ..."

and the other deal with the moon:

"...moonlight carves
The course to follow, a blazing, narrowing scar."

The Shadow phase is also related to the acceptance of the female side of man's psyche. This acceptance is usually experienced in sexual terms. Definite sexual elements can be found in this phase in the poems "The Day of the Statue" and "Serenade to the Favourite Movie-Actress" which will be examined further on. Oblique sexual references can be traced in "For Ethel"(p.135), who seems the name of a woman Webb has known while in Canada. In "Morgan's Country"(p.122) Webb anthropomorphizes the "cave" into the "mother", a benign figure because it provides shelter to Morgan, but not particularly cheerful: she has "...bones/Rattling in her throat when she speaks". "The Day of the Statue"(p.121) is a peculiar poem in which Webb deals with a strange image: the statue, which survives the erosion of the sea and emerges after centuries in the nets of the fishermen.

The symbolic associations are far too clear: the sea-water, a female symbol, is turned into a mouth with "iron gums", which calls to mind a vagina; the statue is described as "A bronze youth, moulded as lyric or a prayer/But mocked by the sea, deformed in his great sheet", the male phallic symbol. In the poem there is one line which is particularly revealing in this case, and which describes the statue lying on the planks of the ship: "sprawled like a scar on the mottled flesh of planks". And as a male symbol when related to the sea - "the ketch nosed down/To the long lunge of the swell" - when looked at from the inside becomes the image of a womb sheltering man from the dangers of the sea.

Thus the line quoted above conveys the feeling of pain occurring in the act of giving birth: if we reconstruct the synecdoche, the line becomes "her legs sprawled her vagina like a scar in (on) the mottled flesh of her (p)flanks". The statue emerging or born and brought to light on the ship after "dull centuries of pressure and lust of weeds" is portrayed further on as "The mortal, the living token"(p.122).

Thus the male and the female elements of the imagery in the poem are intermingled in order to affirm man's power to overcome the eroding and gradually annihilating power of the sea, the symbol for the unconscious and for the female side of the psyche. Nonetheless, at this stage, the statue is still "a mortal living token": in other words, Webb has not yet been able to overcome the destructive powers of his unconscious.

"Serenade to the Favourite Movie-Actress"(p.124) is Webb's only poem fully devoted to a woman; the actress is referred to as a capitalized "Night", whose hands "smooth down all passions". In the poem, the presence of the woman is almost substituted, however only from the third stanza onward, by that of the hound "Beethoven" - a sort of voyeur – which is gradually turned into a phallic symbol in the fourth stanza, where Webb paraphrases an intercourse. And the final stanza reproposes the image of water: "...our kiss/Is a screen of water shaken, an abyss/Opened"(p.48).

As said previously, this phase is characterized by a regression into the unconscious and by Webb's attempt to situate the elements of his imagery in a half-way dimension, balanced between two opposite poles.

In "Dawn Wind on the Islands"(p.141) the contraposition of life/death, night/day, consciousness/unconscious is reconciled by the image of dawn. But this process is depicted again as a painful and excruciating experience. The opening lines of the poem are very significant:

"The needle of dawn has drugged them, life and death,
Stiff and archaic, mouldering into one,"

The state of being suspended between the opposites is not regarded as desirable or safe: the metaphor has clear negative overtones. Webb seems to fear the impact with reality, with consciousness, represented this time by the sun:

".... When
The puppet sun jerks up, there will be no
Convergence: the dead will be the dead."

The mocking sun will unveil all illusions, revealing reality in its crudeness. As a matter of fact, the state of being suspended implies a painful feeling(p.142):

"... If
The point of daylight balances, controls
The sense of life-and-death as on a gaff,
Then dripping it will come, and living...
....
While the moon dies on its branches like a leaf;"

In the final metaphor the poet expresses his sorrow and sadness for the death of the sailors of a ship sunk by a bomber. Webb's wish to immortalize the dead sailors is again turned into a metaphor denouncing the devastating action of the sun:

".... weirs
Of time will burst, burying them; the sunday
Casually mock a cross of stars."

The association of time with sun, and both "mock" the cross of stars with its ambivalent meaning as Southern Cross and as Christ's cross, forecasts the central role of Christian symbolism in Webb's mature poetry. Except that now Webb has not yet accepted fully a Christian vision of life: he still oscillates, as in this poem, between the need of sharing and immortalizing the sad memory of the dead sailors, while at the same time he keeps on searching for a halfway dimension which could save the sailors and himself from the crude reality of the antithesis of life and death. Dawn should last to infinity, day and sunshine should be stopped from coming.

But this intermediate dimension seems much closer to death than to life: apart from the escapism expressed in the first two lines of the poem, the spatial dimension is an island, and the reference at the end of the first stanza to the flight of gulls has also a similar connotation. These components exemplify the state in which Webb's psyche is entrapped: the escape from the outer world into the unconscious will be followed by a desperate search for a metaphysical dimension, in which to take shelter from the reality of his condition.

Another important image/symbol emerging from these poems is sleep: Webb relates it to the desire to go beyond consciousness and the unconscious, and to reconcile the contradiction involved in the experience of the opposites. Sleep is referred to in these terms in "The Gunner"(p.140) where Webb speaks of "the perils of sleep"; whereas in "A View of Montreal"(p.146) sleep carries a positive connotation(p.147):

".... perhaps I strove
Only for this: that sleep become a haspless door,
As now – a wakefulness!

In this poem Webb reports through his persona the voyage if Jacques Cartier to discover Canada. The dream-motif associated with sleep is obviously a familiar one to poets like Webb who base much of their imagery on the material emerging from the unconscious. Section IV of the poem adds a further element to the understanding of the context(p.155):

"... Now and Then,
Past, present, distance, nearness, involved –
Brusque bearings within the toadying cottages when
Mere sleep must pass, mere distance be dissolved;
Itself a darkness, squeezing that true today
From which the piece of wreckage scrambles away.

The myth-making process through which the poet immortalizes dead sailors or dead explorers is in itself a matter of survival for the poet's psyche. To overcome the disruptive action of time, of the sea and sand which annihilates the memory – and not merely the body – of these people, represents for Webb a guarantee of survival from the devastating powers of his unconscious.

This is particularly the case with "On First Hearing a Cuckoo"(p.137). The poem is centered on the synesthetic combination of a sound, the cuckoo's double note, and of a colour, green, which slowly becomes an all-embracing symbol of the poem. The structure of the poem hinges on the interplay between the "two unchanging words" of the cuckoo, "quite apart" and neutral, "but making distant", and the green advancing and enhancing its import in it: hence the former plays in the background, while the latter increases in the foreground.

Webb bridges the gap with the psychic dimension of the poem by abstracting green from the realm of sleep, which seems to have generated it – where he speaks of "the sleepier green than sleep" - and assigns it to a place beyond sleep, to a sort of metaphysical dimension. He also differentiates it from consciousness:

"... Not consciousness, the awakening early green:
For that was the steep curtain, immediate
Structure of pain and learning,"

In the third stanza, where green has almost completely invaded the scenery, the two words are described as being "Never at odds with self, never with green"(p.139), emphasizing again the divergent sensations annexed to sound and colour. In the fourth stanza the poem converges on a scene in a park with the statue of a lekythos. The waning light of the setting sun dissolves distances and there is only one thing left, the two changeless words, and "cool before the cavernous/Green of sleep which alone could lose them".

The structure of the poem is by now hardly detectable unless we translate the significance of its key elements: the poet's self seems to be experiencing the world of physical and everchanging sensations and perceptions, that is to say, his spatial/temporal dimensions, as if through a screen of "green". The reference to the statue in the part has particular cogency in this context: Webb's self is petrified, he is like an actor who watches himself live as if he were another person, who sees his life through a screen of green colour. From this state of alienation he is called back to consciousness by the cuckoo's voice, the two words.

But the sound is not on the same wave-length as the poet's consciousness; and the colour has gone beyond the realm of perceptions into a sort of metaphysical dimension. In other words, the poem seems to reaffirm Webb's intention to refrain from reality. In the last stanza he regards himself as a "a dead word-haunted man"; and the poem ends with the interfusion of the two words, the sound, with a "loose warbling green", in a dream-like world where the unconscious expunges all diversities.

2.3 The Quest for a Metaphysical Dimension

The quest for a metaphysical dimension where all distinctions are effaced is the leading theme of Webb's mature poetry. In order to stand the conflicts generated by his personality, Webb has balanced his self dangerously between two opposite poles, but this experience becomes too painful. The regression into the unconscious carries as a first consequence the representation through the imagery of a private symbolic world. This does not mean that his poems are mere unconscious utterances, devoid of self-sufficiency in literary terms. Obviously every creative act implies a conscious organization of the poetic material – and Webb's poetry shows a mastery in technical and rhetorical devices which is hardly disputable. My point is that the choice of living fully his inner life will eventually bear upon his poetic themes and language.

Significantly enough, the development of his personality as a social or "normal" human being will gradually be prejudiced both spatially and temporally by his life in the asylum. Hence his poems will deal with a limited range of topics; hence his language will become more and more a private language, dependent on his unconscious world, the only one he can rely on for his creative expression. In this sense I shall speak of a "personal myth" in his later poetry, where metaphor is the most characteristic feature.

The motif of the quest, epitomized in the reference to the Dantesque voyage of Ulysses beyond the gates of Herakles, is clearly interwoven with the image of the thirsty Christ on the cross, in "A View of Montreal"(p.149) section one:

"But remains the white tower of our Service
Whereto all words must aspire; therefore, in concluding,
I counsel them not to belittle the good intention:

For while thirst is a rasp whetted on the bitter
Coarse salt of the sea ....
".... while hunger and disease
Are, when we come to them, pain and there is nothing
Nothing but pain, neither truth nor good nor evil."

Webb's three major themes: the exploration theme, the Christ theme and the dimension of madness appear for the first time in the same poem here, which can be regarded as one of his major poems. The realization that pain and suffering are the only reality in life is linked to the presence of the Christ-motif in the following metaphor:

"Let a ship be taken by the ice, squeezed in the scrawny
Fingers of the frozen element, clasped, and racked, and splintered,
Driven like a living nail into the heaving bloodless
Face of the cold and clenched there."

The image of the ship "driven like a living nail" evokes the crucifixion, and the metaphor "face of the cold" evokes the coldness of death; Christ is then, referred to explicitly as the "King", and in the following line, anagogically, as "the honest tree", where the image of the tree is a metonymy for the Cross[29], and the Cross is a metonymy for Christ.

The quest for a metaphysical dimension is on a first level related to the mythopoeic process of memory, which keeps alive the sailor's feats; on a second level it is represented by the search for separateness in section IV, a result of Webb's feelings of seclusion nourished for a society which he regards, and which regards him, as different. The persona – the "I" of the poet – climbs a mountain and feels at a loss "under the whistling unfigured electric Cross"(p.65); the action of

---

[29] see *Acts* 5,30; 10,39; etc.

climbing is expressed, in the first line of this section, by an infinitive and by an impersonal verb: to use indefinite tenses in the syntax corresponds to a rejection of defining temporal dimensions, and confers a durable aspect, a mythic continuity on the action fixed in its archetypal repetition. The first stanza is an extended metaphor of Webb's identification with the myth of Christ and with his role as a Christ-like figure.

In the fourth stanza he broadens his field of connotations by referring, for the first time, to madness: the "cold wiry madman"(p.154) is the embodiment *par excellence* of the misfit, the outcast, his own predicament. The picture is completed by the cogency of the first three lines in the sixth stanza, which exemplify Webb's existential condition with a series of metaphors:

"Designs of distance are false.
There is a will Far from the will of death or treacherous peace,
Slung in the very gimbals of unease."

The span of time intervening before 1953, date of the publication of *Birthday*, Webb's third book of verse, registers the end of his "normal" life in the society of "normality". In 1953 he left Australia for Canada and sailed to Vancouver: as soon as he disembarked he was taken into a mental hospital, where he went through EST and other "therapeutic" treatments currently used in those institutionalized prisons for different or "deviating" people, called mental hospitals. In those resorts, society made these people realize their difference and their extraneousness from society. He spent three month there, then he was taken back to Australia by his sister, with a nurse escort, and admitted to hospital in Sydney. A lawyer got him out of hospital and he again left the country and went to Dublin, where he intended to work as an agricultural labourer, but he did not get through Customs, and spent two months in a mental hospital. He reported to a doctor that he was inclined to blame this on persecution by Communists. When he left Ireland he went to Birmingham, where he felt restless and broke a store window, as as to get a permanent address. As a result of what he said in court, he went into Winson Green Mental Hospital for a period of two months. He then went to stay with an aunt in Epsom for a few weeks; he felt he could not write, was again restless and went wondering in Kent. At Maidenhead in Kent he was again picked up and had a short stay in a mental hospital. When he left there, he found a job with B.B.C., where he did production work, and wrote radio plays.

The poems included in Birthday show the indisputable sign of a fully mature poet: the mastery of a wide vocabulary, the presence of a consistent imagery accompanied by a self-confidence in the substantialization of metaphorical processes, the use of tropes and rhetorical figures. Besides, Webb's self-reliance in dealing with a wide variety of themes is directly linked to his awareness of belonging already to the society of different people, stigmatized as deviating, or labeled as "mentally ill"; certainly commiserable and pitiable people as the personal memoirs contained in the special issue on Webb of *Poetry Australia* already cited clearly shows. These components in Webb's life lead to a gradual but steady transfusion of his whole existential dimension into his poetry, so that his identity as a poet will become all-comprehensive, pervaded by his identity as a man locked inside his own group and outside society, except for his poetic creations.

This displacement of conflicts, frustrations and expectations from the real and everyday world, where they originate and where they cannot be coped with, let alone fulfilled, starts up a process in Webb's psyche. His poetry will become the means to sublimate his psychic needs and to compensate for the repression, oppression and violence endured in his relations with the exterior world. The interior world will then be given the role of receptacle of dreams and fantasies of self-realization, which will be harboured in the unconscious and poured out in the poetic creation. In particular, the awareness of being a person rejected in the body and in the mind, and accepted only through the medium of words on paper will contribute feelings of alienation and extraneousness and will push the poet to search for a different reality in a metaphysical and spiritual world, that is in religion.

In "The Canticle"(p.167) Webb focuses on the double aspect of St Francis' personality, both as a Christ-like figure and as a social misfit, as the chosen and as the socially different, both aspects being epitomized by the stigmata. In the sequence, Webb gathers around the protagonist a series of personae, which represent all the various aspects building up St Francis' multiform world. The Leper represents suffering, pain, the sickness of life: he is equated with the wall surrounding Assisi which can be climbed or crashed down only through the love of a human being. The Father represents order, law and traditions which have to be transgressed in order to be modified. The Wolf of Gubbio is the embodiment of the animality of life, of instinct to be kept under control. The Jongleur, the Knight, and the Serf represent St Francis' society which through conversion, will become part of his new society. The Ass is the personification of poverty and of mildness and acceptance, St Francis' principal virtues.

The key-symbol of the poem is however the sun: it first appears as the "sun-disc", then as

"New sun, round symbol
Blown to us
Wind-ferried, humble,
Mountainous."(p,169)

as "a purse-paring of sunlight"(p.170); in

"delicate rains
Give point to the sun's face"(p.175);

capitalized in "the nonplussed look of the Sun"(p.181); in assonance with "son" in "From dead twilight fibres coaxes a sun"(p.184); here the transfiguration of St Francis at La Verna is described by the image of a transcendent light piercing the night, which is paralleled by the stigmata, an attribute of Christ. This association with Christ has transfigured the symbols of light and the sun; besides, what was previously defined as a painful piercing of the unconscious by consciousness has also acquired another layer of meaning: in the perspective of the myth of Christ pain and suffering are the premises for the resurrection theme.

In "Tallis to Vaughan Williams"(p.201) Webb widens the scope of his imagery through a further and deeper layer of associations: he links the sun-Christ symbol to the natural processes of death and rebirth exemplified by the image of the tree. The realm of nature, of the seasons, of death, life and rebirth is explored in the first stanza of the poem. The refrain focusses on the poet's wish to be "at one" with the natural world. But in the second line this wish acquires a mythico-religious features: "one" is made to rhyme with "sun" and phonetic interaction suggests the word "son", through a semantic interference, as was the case with "The Father"(p.183) in "The Canticle".

The anaphoric construction of the last two lines proposes a parallel structure but an opposed content: "oldness" is defined with a definite marker, whereas "newness" has an indefinite one. Webb's wish for oneness with the natural world is linked with his intention of atonement, of redemption, and is closely connected to his awareness of the need to shed the body in view of a spiritual rebirth - a "newness" burning. The spiritual dimension of rebirth is strongly emphasized in the final line of the second stanza, where Webb speaks of "the crying and laughter of a child"(p.202), which actualizes the intimation of rebirth reiterated by the refrain. The presence of the oxymoron, a figure of speech which conveys the unity of opposites, draws our attention to the fact that Webb is keenly aware of the suffering involved by this unity, which recalls the myth of Christ.

The metaphysical quest is gradually channeled, then, into the wish for renewal and rebirth: the title itself given to this book corroborates this idea. Further, the few poems dealing with marine or nautical themes do not tell of shipwrecks but of discovery; particularly in "Vlamingh and Rottnest Island"(p.90), the exploration theme is associated with Christmas in the opening line "always, forever, a Morning and a Coming", and the sailors are visualized as "Magi of a kind".

2.4 Rebirth and Alienation

This feeling of rebirth is also suggested by the fourfold structure of some of the poems in this book, a tendency which will become paramount in *Socrates*: the quaternity is a Jungian symbol for the Self, paralleled by Christ, another symbol of the Self; both symbols are emerging in *Birthday*. We find them in "Galston"(p.85) a poem where the fourfold structure is also emphasized by the presence in each poem of the sequence of one of the four elements: fire, air, earth, water, in that order. In the first poem the bush-fire is set against the darkness of the night and is dramatized by the anthropomorphic description of nature. In the second poem the imagery is reversed: the blackness of the cockatoos is now set against the redness of the sun.

Webb interweaves these contrasting images with the image of blue sky and both are interfused in a reference to Christ, as the eucharist, with "the cloth and the cap"(p.86). The metaphysical dimension is also hinted at by a reference to music "unearthly as space itself". These references are reinforced in the third stanza which speaks of the miracle of grace transfused into nature by the sacrifice of Christ on the cross, of which the mass is a ritual reiteration. The fourth poem is staged against a background of sleep and night and water: the dimension of sleep is connected to the leit-motif of "waiting". The sensation that one gets from the sequence as a whole is conditioned by the reference to grace and to the redeeming function of the eucharist, in the second poem, while the final poem contributes a sense of being suspended, waiting for something to happen, for someone to come and to give meaning with its being to the poem's life.

In "Laid-Off", "The Stations", "The Song of a New Australian", and partly in "Birthday", Webb comes to grips with the condition of alienated people, stigmatized by their difference, secluded from the society of normality - a condition which was starting to become his own personal experience. In "The Stations"(p.208) the drama of the oppressed, the person disqualified from social acceptance, is compared with Christ's Calvary, set on the stage of Glebe. Webb depicts the inhabitants of the suburb as the Pharisees slandering with "Immigrant words", like "The dirty dagoes, the rats"(p.95) the Christ-labourer-immigrant, carrying his cross: the time dimension is Lent, the Friday before Easter.

The poet, at first, identifies himself with the neighbours in the line "Someone is told to die. We told him this."; then, he seems to partake of the same predicament as the Christ-labourer-immigrant in

"... They will redeem
Themselves, redeem me. But the wood is cruel to the back."

Eventually, the personae are all interfused in the passion of Christ, redeeming their sins and the sins of mankind with his sacrifice on the cross. The two final stanzas are based on pure oxymora, or on the combination of opposed semantic fields: "At this ruthless curve/We are driven to live"; Sydney is portrayed as a "city/Of glory and torment - human", "this spearhead of gall/Touches the tongue of new life"; "Always this coffin is rather the flower's closing". The interfusion of the social and the individual is accomplished at the end with the lines,

"... Sunset hails a raising.
The eve of Resurrection is in this room.

In "The Song of a New Australian"(p.213) Webb explores the theme of alienation in his society. The poem is full of metaphors conveying the core of this condition: "In the hamper of a fictive world", "hideous mockery of loving", "Cannot have me in his black book, Mateship", "so I fall/Like the other thousand mile-torn goods, to the phrases/Of the account-book", where the poet's words are turned into objects to be sold and bought. This process of reification, strangely enough, resembles very closely the Marxist theory of alienation (even though Webb believed he was persecuted by communists). Thus he externalizes his awareness of living his object-like alienated life in a society which generates alienation.

In this society, the state of being normal corresponds to the degree of alienation the individual is willing to stand in order to survive "breakdowns": we can surmise that Webb was unwilling, let alone unable, to undergo and endure the stress determined by the pressures of society which he didn't appreciate. Consequently, labeled as a mentally ill person - and as "paranoid schizophrenic" in particular - he accepted to be locked for reasons of security in mental hospitals, where therapeutic treatments had the aim to help people recover and manage to return to be part of the society of "normality".

Madness in this phase is related to the theme of the outcast, the misfit in "Birthday"(p.219): this radio-play is apparently centered on the theme of Hitler's death, but the poet's major concern is the justification of madness. The play opens with the Speaker's oblique remark on Hitler's madness in the line

"Admittedly, the psychiatrist's weekly metaphor
Will coldshoulder that of the public bar"

which is counterpointed by the statement at the end, "Hitler was a human being"(p.221). The central character of the play is the figure of Hans, the German Guard, who was driven mad and killed by Morell, one of the Nazi doctors who used to make experiments on the brains of human beings. Webb scatters references to him in the play: at first with the Speaker, who emphatically comments "Hans was more than a man"(p.230); then, through the words of Hans, speaking in first person (p.228; p.230); then, through Goebbels'(p.237) and Goering's(p.243) descriptions of their acquaintance with him; and finally Hitler's last words before his death are dedicated to Hans(p.256).

Inside the play, Webb obliquely relates this aspect to racism, and to the discrimination worked on

"Dagoes, Wogs, and Dings,
And similar dross."(p.230)

The aspects of alienation and reification are completely lacking in *Socrates* but will reappear in *The Ghost of the Cock*. In fact, as I pointed out at the beginning of the chapter, Webb's poetry cannot be divided merely on a thematic level; on a closer look, *Socrates* reveals a development in Webb's view of reality realized solely on the grounds of modifications introduced into the poetic language. One can roughly affirm that *Socrates* shows, quantitatively speaking, an enormous increase in metaphorical processes: but the quality of the language in, say, "Eyre All Alone", is remarkably different from that of "A Death at Winson Green"; and this is different from that of "Five Days Old".

Generally speaking, one could say that there is a predilection for metaphors on anthropomorphic representations of nature: but the mythic personification of, say, *Socrates* is definitely in texture and scope from that of "October". The same arguments could be applied to the formal structure of the poems: one has to differentiate between verse patterns, internal rhymes, alliterations, assonances and other rhetorical figures and tropes present in the poems written in 1954-56 and those written in 1957-59. These differences will be taken care of by the Computational Analysis described in Chapter VI. From the various phases in *Socrates* I shall try to delineate the development in Webb's *Weltanschaung*.

CHAPTER III: TOWARDS THE CREATION OF A PERSONAL MYTH

3.1 The sacred illness and the Myth of Christ

Socrates is Webb's most conspicuous poetic achievement. It covers a time-span of eight years, which were spent mostly in mental hospital, and particularly at Norwich Mental Hospital in Norfolk, as a voluntary patient. This is by far Webb's best single book, as far as poetic inspiration and technical achievements are concerned. It seems, then, that the heightening in creative activity is counterpoised by a gradual deterioration of his mental "health" in this perspective - the one proposed by institutionalized science - the possibility of finding a point of contact between "normality" and poetic creativity becomes inevitably a very loose and chancy fact.

In *Birthday* Webb's poetry was advancing towards a more and more metaphysical and spiritual dimension. This is particularly true for *Socrates* and this can be related to two important factors. Webb was relegated by society into those peculiar lagers which are mental hospitals - he was advised by a BBC producer to enter Norwich hospital. His wish to transfigure reality into a spiritual, but immanent, realm was dictated by his belief in the mediating figure of Christ, who was becoming his answer to his predicament. From a reading of *Socrates*, it becomes apparent that Webb does not put any particularly direct blame on society for his condition: he rather seems to be convinced of the fact that both his creativity and his human condition are to be understood as something bestowed from above.

The role of the poet is thus envisaged as a segregating fact in itself, to be accepted as a cross, and as a divine grace at the same time, in

Christian terms. Life in Webb's perspective has to be understood as a reiteration of a myth, the myth of Christ.

"Electric"(p.326) could have been written at the time of his hospitalization in Canada, or shortly after, while in England, about 1953, when he was given electroshock therapy. The most interesting part of the play is the "Epilogue"(p.345), where he refers to madness as the "sacred illness" and relates it to the myth of Christ. The poem is built on a succession in the imagery which dramatizes the myth of Christ by a series of antinomies, interwoven with one another. This progressing structure is interoperated with the reiteration of the "sacred illness" in the last line of each quatrain. This is reconciled through language to the myth of Christ in the second-last stanza, by the use of "forgiven" and of the passive form, as well as by the parallelism introduced with "the electric cross". Thus the last stanza affirms the necessity for everyman to "clasp to his soul/The sacred illness".

The somewhat moral tinge of the imagery seems to imply that this poem might have been added to the rest of the play only later on, possibly in 1960. Images are centred around two semantic clusters of associations: the opposition of "sun" and "truth", and the relatedness of "pain", "Cross", "illness". This is done by means of a network of clausal objective correlatives, such as "gold", "black", "dawn"; as by the metaphor "the gold doorway of dawn" in the first quatrain, which is paralleled by "the black doorway of our curse" in the fourth quatrain.

The intention of the poet is again that of combining opposite poles in order to affirm the necessity of accepting and justifying pain, sin, and illness in view of the redeeming function of the myth of Christ. To this end the poem's formal pattern also works. Webb has introduced a sort of intertwined rhyme scheme, which contributes that effect: beside the last line of each stanza, which is a sort of refrain, there is a pure rhyme in the fourth line of each quatrain which conveys, through the reiteration of its sound, a sort of leit-motif, a fixed standpoint in the total structure.

The second line of each quatrain is also used as a link: "carven", "woven", "forgiven", "cloven" are all threaded through the rhyme pattern which is lighted in its sound effect by the first and third line of each quatrain organized on an alliterative scheme with an internal consonance carefully arranged: the couples "dawn"/"down", "stone"/"stain" fade into an alliteration in "loom"/"limbs" and "curse"/"Cross", turning into an assonance and a consonance in "assail" and "soul", but also "dawn" and "soul". Worth noting here is also the use of monosyllabic words, which enhances the semantic impact of the poem and is in contrast to the iterative rhythm contrived by the rhymes.

On a more complex patterns of images is based "A Death at Winson Green"(p.302), which focuses again on the association of the myth of Christ with the theme of mental illness. In this poem the ward is transfigured into a church, and the death of the madman is turned into a resurrection. The time dimension of the poem is marked out by the progress of the sun during the day: morning, in the first two stanzas, is followed by noon in the third; evening and twilight in the fourth and night in the fifth. This descending pattern is in contrast to the ascending one connected to the spiritual dimension, which culminates in the rebirth foreshadowed by the inmate death. In fact the poem's imagery is also built on a network of metaphors based on opposed semantic fields, linked together by the central theme of death-rebirth:

1st stanza:

> "for the treacherous lord
> of time, the dazed historic sunlight, must
> .....
> Quake like foam on the lip, or lie still as the dead."

2nd stanza:

> "the graven perpetual smile,
> a beauty which we hate and love.
> The reminiscent feast-day, long
> since dead."(p.303)

3rd stanza:

> "and a man is dying at the core
> Of triumph won.
> As a tattered, powerful wing
> The screen"

4th stanza:

> "Inviolate, faithful as a saint he lies
> Twilight itself breaks up, the venal ship,
> Upon the silver integrity of his face.
> Unmarked, unmoving, from the gaping bed
> Toward birth he labours, honour, almost dead."

5th stanza:

> "... his burden grows
> Heavier as all earth lightens, and all sea.
> He is all life, thrown on the gaping bed.
> Blind, silent, in a trance, and shortly, dead."

    The succession of these contrasting metaphoric units has involved all creation in the progressing movement of the poem: from death in the ephemeral sphere of human life to the birth of the spiritual being. The dialectical intersection of these elements is emphasized in the last stanza by the reiteration of "all", and in the final couplet of the rhyme-scheme which works as a leit-motif inside the poem. Besides the anthropomorphic representations of nature, Webb personifies also the urban landscape: the "peering omnibus" looks over the fence; "apathetic pillars" plot the ward; "Tired timbers wheeze and settle into dust". In these metaphors he seems to look for a separation between the outer world, with the "heathens" coming to visit the inmates, and the inner world of the ward, where all creation is assembled around the bed of the dying-resurrecting patient.

In the fourth stanza he comments: "Traffic and factory-whistle turn berserk" and "No bread shall tempt that fine, tormented lip"; in other words, the ward and the inmate are projected against a mythico-religious background, in order to set it apart from everyday life. Significantly enough, Webb's world is from now on that of the ward: thus madness is "a sacred illness"; and, as he says in "The Chalice", "Come into a hospital - here are miracles"(p.304)

The transfiguration of Webb's surroundings is related to another and complementary transfiguration in his inner world. The dialectical movement from death to resurrection dramatized by the inmate-Christ persona is reflected by another rebirth in the poet: "I sleep as a child, rouse up as a child might" he says in "A Death at Winson Green". The symbol of the child,, which is a recurrent one both in *Socrates* and in *The Ghost of the Cock*, is a highly revealing symbol of Webb's psychic life: to transcend death, in symbolic terms, corresponds to a victory over the unconscious, over the night; it is also a victory over the dimension of sleep, another meeting point of opposites.

In psychological terms, Webb has now reached the point where the unconscious becomes a positive element in the life of the psyche and helps to bring about the creative function of the feminine elements in his unconscious. In the poem Webb has introjected the process of death and rebirth and feels inside himself as if he were bearing a child, a psychic child. This is due foremost to the acceptance of his feminine side, and to his conjunction with it. Thus the attainment of the totality of the psychic life is borne out in symbolic terms by the generation of the psychic child. On a metaphysical level Webb is now projecting himself beyond the opposites which are reconciled in a spiritual dimension.

"The Chalice"(p.304) another radio play provides a landmark for his poetic work as a whole, thanks to its wealth of symbolic associations, each one set in different spatial and temporal dimensions. I shall concentrate on the analysis of the first section, which is set in the Rome of the third century. Here Webb devotes himself to the mythical recreation of the primitive Christian underworld of the catacombs. The imagery hinges on three main clusters of symbolic associations: "the chalice", "blood", originating in their union the metaphysical "light" of rebirth. Most metaphors are based on the anthropomorphic portrayal of nature: Webb's language seeks to attain an identification of self and nature through a mythic projection of the data of experience which carry unconscious associations.

The anthropomorphism in Webb is basically a projection of his inner conflicts, of his emotions and sensations: through it, he calls for participation of the cosmic forces and presences in his existential drama, namely in the struggle of his unconscious with consciousness. This fusion of man and nature denotes the persistence of a symbolist view of the world, where everything is organically connected, and the representation of the real is open to a series of arbitrary events deprived of casual nexus.

The union of the chalice, a clear feminine symbol, with Christ's blood, is reiterated in the union of the earth with the setting sun: the mountain is depicted as a breast, drinking "with large stone eyes agape", while its "wasted blue flesh takes on veins and rumours of colours" of the sunset. The community of Christians lives inside the earth, in a sort of foetal womb: they are neither alive nor dead. The catacombs are called "caverns of burial under sundown" and the sunset is a "healing draught".

The symbolic associations are now starting to come to light: the womb, the chalice containing and absorbing the male symbol of the sun, the blood of the Saviour, Christ, is meant to bring to light the redeeming psychic child of redemption. The *hieros gamos*, or the sacred mythopoeic union of the two opposite sexual symbols is structured by the anthropomorphic representation of nature, on a symbolic and, then, anagogic level, particularly in St Peter's words "the Last Supper of all daylight the colour of blood".

Christ is the "Lover" and "sunset/Is the cry of my mother in giving birth to me", where the synesthesia renders perfectly the sexual union of the opposites: female and male, light and dark, the red sun and the black womb of the night/earth bearing the child of rebirth and resurrection, the transfiguring spiritual vision denied to the Christians living in catacombs, as well as to the man living in the darkness of the unconscious, a foetus living in the womb, as Webb puts it:

"We are denied the vision
Of sun on water, childbearing, light darkness"

It is the love of Christ, as Peter says:

"I am to tell you
Of all light, all love, fast to the Cross, and bleeding"

The metaphors of the early Christians in catacombs is extended in the last section, when we enter the hospital world of the inmates, where people are being persecuted by the outer world; the return to the womb of the earth in the catacombs is opposed here to the condition of the "mentally ill" people in hospitals, literally uprooted from a life on a conscious level, and obliged to a regression into the dark realm of the unconscious where they should recapture their lost integrity. The other anthropomorphic metaphors completing the net of associations linked to the nodal images and symbols of the play are contained in the following sections, namely in section three, where we have a

> "... Tower, breast rose moodily
> In the embrace of a steep spousal blue before dawn"(p.312)

and further on, where the mountain, at first called "eternity"(p.315) is "the mother, has the mother power". The play ends in a mental hospital, where the wife of a dead airman transfigures the death of the man she loves in that of Christ, the Lover: in the last two stanzas the aeroplane's wings become the "wings of a dove"(p.324) announcing the rebirth and resurrection of her husband thanks to her love. "Peace", "war", "joy", "pain" are joined and reconciled through the myth of Christ: the husband's death is equalled to the death of Christ, the lover.

3.2 The union of the opposites with Christ

With the poem "Light"(p.281) Webb realizes the transformation of the image of light, from a symbol of painful strife in the psyche into a symbol of rebirth. This poem accounts for Webb's endeavour to attain peace, harmony, and order, while encompassing the antinomies of life. It deals on a symbolic level, with the rising of the sun and dramatizes the victory of light over darkness. This process is not carried out in terms of a manichean opposition, as is the case with other Australian poets - McAuley for instance. Webb deals with light as if it were the natural offspring of darkness.

Light is, then, identified with Christ: hence the rising of the sun is eventually equated with Christ's resurrection. Psychological connotations are added to the symbol of light by another layer of meaning: Webb dramatizes through the birth of light from darkness his interior process of rebirth from the destructive and overwhelming power of the unconscious. This internalization of experience actualized his attainment of the process of individuation, <u>the light of the Self</u>. Webb introduces a series of liturgical words without overcharging it: thus, we have "doctrine", "vow", "grace", "oratory", "true disc" in the first stanza; "libation" in the second stanza; "candle and basin", "secret credo and ark" in the third stanza; "pilgrimage", "honour", and "tablet" in the fourth stanza. In addition each stanza is closed by a line-refrain based on the rising-resurrecting theme.

The rising of the mythic sun-God Christ from darkness lends its meaning to the first anthropomorphic level of the central metaphor of the poem: all life and creation is, thus involved in the progress of the imagery towards rebirth. For instance, the passage from the darkness of the night to the light of the day in the first stanza is associated with a reference to the seasons, in the second stanza, "he may ponder the April mist". There is also a continual presence of the time-dimension: "Time labours towards a meaning upon the wrist", "Coxcombry ot time? the clock tower ticks by its lone". The quality of the metaphoric language in this poem is a peculiar mixture of early and later materials, combined together in a more complex context. In the opening lines there is a synesthetic image,

"great stone lips set in vow
Of colour, words, oratory of birds"

a device peculiar to this phase, which is associated with a metaphor in nautical language, "Bladed golden oars haul the true disc". In the second stanza the metaphor based on the idea of sacrifice is an asyndetic line peculiar to this phase, "Before day swallows, ingests him, offers libation": which is reinforced by an anthropomorphic metaphor derived from a previous phase, "A ploughshare might plot moon-courses over the plains". The continuity of the language is accounted for by Webb's psychological development and certainly not by a regression in his "mental illness".

A critical analysis of a poem as complex and as beautiful as "From the Cold"(p.277) is in no way to be regarded as an attempt to "explain" the poem, nor is it to be intended as a reduction of it in the meta-language of prose. The poem gives few indications as to a theme: the heaviest weight as to its content is carried forward by the imagery, and by rhetorical figures. One could venture to define it as a poem on the reproduction of natural life: this first reference points in the second part to the Passion of Christ. One could speak, then, of a transfiguration of natural life and renewal by the myth of Christ. The first part of the poem depicts the stage in which all life is imprisoned in ice and coldness. But the apparent death-like transparency of ice foreshadows the outburst of life in the second part, particularly in the last line: "The birdform and pulse of quickening morning light".

The second part opens with a reference to a river flowing to the ocean's belly, a metaphor for the end of the incubation of all life-forms in the grip of ice. The second stanza introduces the motif of the tree, a symbol of life and a metonymy for Christ. This reference is enlarged in the ending couplet of the poem which reaffirms the beginning of natural life through "coral" in the sea and "wheat" on the earth. The poem as a whole is then an extended metaphor of the phenomenon of the creation of life from an amorphous and shapeless primordial stage.

Going back to the first stanza, we can notice Webb's concern with assembling as many epithets as he can this orderless and ill-defined accumulation of images belonging to diverse semantic domains, of abstract and concrete derivation, is a juxtaposition of subjective emotional connotations which give the idea of a state of chaos on a psychic level. The subsequent reduction of the adjectives, especially in part two, accounts for his intention to communicate the passage from the darkness of the beginnings, to the illumination of life by means of Christ's redeeming presence.

The quality of the metaphors, which are mainly anthropomorphic, is also a revealing feature: there is only one simile mediated by "as", the remaining metaphors are direct ones, that is, their different semantic fields overlap and the gap between them has been completely erased. Significantly enough, the simile is included in the second part, "time as a secret bell is trembling", and has again a synesthetic effect. The simile denotes the poet's intention to remain distinct and separate from the contents of his poetic material. On the contrary, the metaphor *tout court* equates all opposites interfusing them in a sort of primordial state of indifference.

This poem shows Webb's intention to convey part of the meaning through the use of rhetorical figures: I am here referring in particular to the anaphora with demonstrative adjectives in part one of the poem. The reiteration of "these" and "this" in the first three lines of the stanza is used as a link with the second stanza and is opposed to the reiteration of "but" in the third line of part two. The anaphora and the parataxis of "This coral, this weed, this man" propose simple successions of noun phrases, avoiding definite syntactic relations between actions and facts; both devices relate the facts of reality or of fantasy with a lack of internal nexus and logical order denoting unrest and search for interior peace. Life is viewed as an amorphous juxtaposition of all forces and elements, as a chaos lacking in an adequate structure.

This attitude is to become paramount in the later poems, particularly in "Mousehold Heath", and in "Eyre All Alone". Worth noting is also Webb's intention to entrust the unifying process in the poem's semantic structure, to coordinating particles such as "but", "or", a rather common feature of this book.

Webb intersperses part one with such key images as "coral" and "weed", which will be turned into "wheat" in the last line of the poem. The first sentence is closed by a double metaphor which contains *in nuce* the basic conflict solved by the poem: "the midnight sun" and "the frozen myth". The association of "bird-form" with "morning light" is also resumed in part two, where Webb refers to a "black swan", "brave singer" and further on to "a bird's voice", until the final couplet where "Out singer" personifies the herald of the rebirth of life.

But the most revealing metaphor is "a tree drinks of moonlight in the garden", which on the one hand is linked to Christ and prefigures the content of the last line of the following stanza, where the scene shifts to Gethsemane and to Christ's "words of choice".

On the other hand, the metaphor is charged with a profound symbolic meaning: the tree-symbolism is here linked to the image of the moon which is represented as a cup or a vessel, a feminine symbol, pouring its light onto the tree branches. If we examine the symbol of the tree, we come at first to acknowledge its mediating function: it mediates between the cthonic underworld of the unconscious which nourishes its roots, and it reaches out from consciousness towards the sky, the air, light and the spiritual realm. Thus the metaphor externalizes Webb's yearning for the conjunction with the *Anima*, the feminine side of the psyche and the archetype bequeathing the totality of the *Self*.

3.3 The opposites and immanence

"Socrates"(p.269) is a poem about immanence: the refrain focuses on the idea of immanence and expresses it in terms of opposites: "dark night" is opposed to "living light"; "light" becomes a metaphysical entity reflecting the "Form", "the immanence", as "the immortal soul". The poem foresees the condition of rebirth as a passage from the world of flesh and ephemeral facts into that of soul and immortality, which cleaves to the former. In other words, Webb shuns the idea of transcendence, of a hiatus, a chasm between the realm of the human in time, and the realm of the divine in eternity.

The opening couplet is based on the same concept: the technique is again the synesthesia which serves Webb's aim of interlocking different entities apparently belonging to separate semantic fields: the personification of "daylight" is thus transformed into a voice calling to birth the lyrical "I" of the poem. The imagery shifts from bearing to sight with the reference to "my pallet", where "the new/ancient voice" dispels the "wheedlings of sleep", as the rising sun dispels the darkness of the night. The complexity of the metaphor can be traced in the unity of hearing and sight, of new and ancient, and merges two time perspectives - present and past; whereas the "wheedlings" of sleep emphasize the suasive and coaxing function of the image of darkness, at the opposite pole of birth and light. The moment of death is treated again as the fulcrum where the descending and ascending structures of the poem converge and coalesce: death in the body corresponds to birth in the soul.

A conspicuous part of the poem is devoted to the idea of sacrifice, which is explored at various levels: for instance, Sisyphus symbolizes the rising and setting of the sun on a mythical level; on a metaphysical level he becomes the embodiment of the passing of time, consequently the alternation of life and death in time. A further level is represented by his being the personification of pain and suffering inherent to human life on earth and in time. Sisyphus is made in this way a symbol akin to Christ, the sun-god who brings redemption by his sacrifice - and Sisyphus' mythological origins can be traced back to a sun-god.

Besides, the idea of sacrifice is also part of Socrates' story, who gave his life in order to affirm his dignity as a human being. The subject has a religious background reflected by the language in the poem, where the epic tone can be traces in the use of iterative patterns, and in the presence of anaphoric procedures, such as the one built on "till" in the fourth stanza. Webb has also scattered in the poem remarkable anthropomorphic metaphors such as: "The long long flutes of the sea"(p.276); "the temple reels like a drunken giant on the plain"; "ocean returns to his nuptials with palebreasted land"; "the sun smiles simply".

Webb's intention to identify himself with Socrates' death, and to turn it into a private and mythic one by means of the Christ archetype can be traced particularly in the shift of the subject from the first person in the quatrain devoted to childhood - at pag. 273 - to the third person in the following quatrain; and again to the first person in the third quatrain, where Webb seems to be re-living Socrates' death. "I confess connivance, weeping, on my knees"(p.274).

The intimation of harmony proceeding from a view of the world based on the idea of immanence has, in my opinion, made it possible for Webb to write such perfectly-wrought poem as "Bells of St Peter Mancroft" and "Five Days Old". The two poems mark out the passage in *Socrates* from a first to a second phase: their structure shows the attainment of an inner self-confidence, an intuition of order and harmony reflected by the outer world. "Bells of St Peter Mancroft"(p.279) is an outburst of mirth, a hymn to life full of pious and religious feelings. Webb does not affirm the supremacy of God as opposed to man, or vice versa: the two beings are at one and perfectly balanced in the structure of the poem, which is at the same time "self-enclosed" and "open", as it were. The self-enclosed feature is traceable in the parallelism between the first and the last life of the poem: "Gay golden volleys of barter" which is coordinated by the central position of "golden" and the alliteration with "Gay". The poem's main parallelisms are constituted by double adjectives in "the old lofty tower", and "the ancient holy eye", reinforcing the starting couple "Gay golden". Then the use of the coordinating "and" in "roll and wink", "blunder and wander", "hale and blest". The internal structure of the poem is paralleled by the external one, which is an "open" structure in that its rhyme-pattern is based on a series of minimal variations in assonances and consonances, contributing through a sort of half-rhymes, an increase in the semantic resonances of the verse, while at the same time leaving the sound-pattern somewhat light and loose.

The same technical devices can be traced in "Five Days Old"(p.298), but in this poem both patterns - the reiteration in the internal structure and the rhyme-scheme in the external one - are introduced as a means of interlocking the stanzas together thus making it into a much more "self-enclosed" poem. In the first stanza we have repetitions of "all" and of superlative forms in "quietest", "loneliest" denoting the exceptionality and all-enclosing effect associated with the poem. In the second stanza two similes based on an anaphoric "so", followed in the third stanza by the parallelism between "humbly and utterly", "bells, bells". Then in the fourth stanza again the presence of double adjectives, and in the fifth and in the last stanza the reiteration of the coordinating particle "and".

In "Hospital Night"(p.325), the poet is again experiencing a sense of longing for a spiritual rebirth, which seems to resume an early theme. In fact, even if the poem is balanced at first between the state of sleep and that of awakening, Webb does not concentrate on the intermediate moment of dawn, or "truce", which appears in most poems of this book, "Sleep" becomes a symbol conveying the idea of the womb, where the foetus of the poet's self is waiting for a second birth: sleep, night, and darkness have been given a painful connotation and the poem is projected towards the image of a star, which shall bring the overcoming of darkness, both in its physical and metaphysical connotations.

The passing of time with its polarized scansion determined by the alternation of night and day, of darkness and light, is also painful. Thus the star, closing the poem, is an intimation of a metaphysical dimension which stems from the interaction of two opposite poles, but which transcends them. Webb conveys the dialectical interplay of the conflicting entities partially through the broken rhythm imposed on the poem; and then through iterative patterns such as: "skyward, nightward" in the first stanza, and in the second stanza:

"Darkness is astir, pondering, touching
Kinship with the first Dark"

In the third stanza we have "my thought is pain,/Pain". Other poetic processes are constituted by charging iterative patterns with a semantic function and by turning the anadiplosis into a double metaphor, as in "faceless jousting of green and green by an old cell", or in "they glitter and glitter of a lover", and in

"For these, isled upon time, are murmuring, murmuring ever
Of good and evil"

The ambivalence of meaning, or the dialectical valency of these compounds is reflected by the introduction of such figures of speech as the oxymoron, in "ice-world summers"; or in the ambiguous use of adverbs in the fourth stanza, where "ever" is opposed to "never" and to "yet". The same devices are used in the last stanza in order to convey the otherworldliness of the "star", which is "near nor far" and echoes the other figure "White notes nor black"; or again by the accumulation of adjectives pertaining to different semantic fields in "frail intense blue burning".

The animistic personification of nature is, then, based on synesthetic compounds such as "trees... rustle forward in the steep time" or "a star is uttered in the long night"; "pitched beyond altercation of tree and storm". It is also worth noting that in this poem, Webb reintroduces the colour "green", which represents sensation in Jungian terms; "blue" on the contrary, the colour annexed to the star in the last stanza of the poem, is linked to creativity.

3.4 Doctors and Judges, Sin and Guilt

In "To a Doctor"(p.283) we find the same spatial dimension, the hospital, of "Hospital Night", but the technique and the language used are much more similar to "A Death at Winson Green". Webb has changed the rhyme-scheme, diminishing the number of lines in each stanza - eight lines instead of ten. In this way the poem gains in conciseness and the rhythm accelerates almost to resemble a ballad. He has threaded through the poem a legal metaphor, which serves him in order to extrapolate his condition as patient-prisoner. The hospital is turned into the court where the inmate must show his evidence and proofs and has to be judged for his illegal behaviour.

The first stanza opens with a metaphor in legal language: "The scales are set", continued in the second hemistich, "all retinue and baggage", where retinue denotes a group of retainers. In the third line "tags" could also be referred to legal language: to tag can mean to charge someone who has violated the law. The fifth line has an explicit reference to "scrawls of judgement" and in the following line Webb introduces the word "sin", as a sign that he not only equates the hospital with a court, but also with a church, as in "A Death at Winson Green". In other words, the inmate entering the hospital is not only guilty of illegal behaviour against society, but also of "sins": the treatment imposed by the doctor/judge will become a sort of redeeming action which is meant to cleanse the inmate of his charges and his sins. This is what Webb says in second stanza, where his spirit is "glued and writhing" on the sticky "wan flypaper course/Of hygienic time": by the end of the stanza the relation doctor/inmate has already been transfigured in religious terms, "Bring/Grace to this world, to all the world, and sing."

Webb's preoccupation with sin is worth commenting on here, since it represents an implicit or explicit all-pervasive motif in *Socrates* and in *The Ghost of the Cock*. Webb's search for the purity of a spiritual life coincides, on the one hand, with a Christian quest; on the other hand, it is linked to his life as a human being secluded in mental hospitals. Webb interrelates the two clues when he tries to "explain" his condition as inmate in terms of sin, which, according to the Christian and Catholic religion, is a contingent, but nonetheless immanent component of the human condition (as the original sin). The Christian/Catholic view of life is tragic in that it is conceived in terms of guilt and atonement: Christ, the saviour, is sent by God to forgive the sins of the whole human kind in the world.

But Webb's identification with this archetypal figure, introjected to the point of becoming his only reality, is set in a different perspective from McAuley's poetry. In this latter case, the oppositions inherent in life were set wide apart and made up his tragic complex, leading to a "Manichean view of life": McAuley was unable to accept the contradictoriness of the human condition, thus life was experienced as a continual war of good against evil, of light against darkness[30]. This is not the case with Webb's dialectical view of life: as it has been shown by the poetry so far, the opposites are always encompassed and from their continual interaction stems a new entity of a spiritual kind, a

---

[30] See my Ph.D. unpublished dissertation cited.

psychic child which symbolizes rebirth.

Webb's condition as inmate leads to a different distortion of the Christian/Catholic doctrine: his world becomes a means of accepting reality, not as it is in the outer world, but as it has been given to him to live by, as an inmate of mental hospitals. His quest for an identity in the religious sphere is, then, marred by the incongruity generated by his life in a reality which has been forced upon him, a false reality and as such falsifying his own legitimate search. Religion becomes, in this context, a means to accept his reality- a womb that shelters him from the other reality of outside society. It is no longer the expression of a free human being wishing a free spiritual union with God. It is rather the expression of an oppressed man who has been obliged, because of his "difference", to create a reality which is meant to solve his inner tensions.

Even though Webb is trapped in a false reality - he no longer attacks society in his poetry as he did in *Birthday* (but maybe he still continues to oppose his society in private conversations). He rejects a passive identification with the myth of Christ, which would mean that he lives it on an unconscious level: his quest for a metaphysical realm where the opposites are encompassed and reconciled, for harmony and order bears witness to this hypothesis. Webb refrains from locking himself up in a world made only of pain and suffering. In this sense the myth of Christ is experienced in its totality: from the stage in which suffering is the only reality, to the stage of resurrection and rebirth in a spiritual realm, immanent and not transcendent. This second stage is symbolized by the motif of the psychic child, which is the essence, the core of his personal myth and the key to understand its later negative modification.

We find it particularly in "Five Days Old"(p.298) where Webb transfigures the child he has been given to hold in his hands, into a Christ child. The poem is important, because it reveals a peculiar sort of identification: the scene in the last two stanzas is set in the stable which saw the birth of Christ. The references to the manger and to the Magi are completed by a reference to the Dove, the Holy Ghost who conceived Christ in Mary's womb. The poet's question, "Tell me what I hold"(p.293), sounds as if Webb has identified himself with the Virgin Mary, questioning the Dove.

In "To a Doctor"(p.283) this identification becomes even stronger: in the third and fourth stanzas he transfigures the relation between the patient and the doctor respectively into that intervening between the Virgin Mary and the Dove of the Holy Spirit. The last stanza describes the celebration of a wedding in a church, with organ music, in an ironic language, which sways from the mocking to the celebrating tone. The doctor is turned into a "Musician, or Angel of Annunciation"(p.284) and into a sexual partner with the reference to "contrapuntal love" and the oxymoron "with painful joy".

For want of a better dating I include "October"(p.346) here: as to its technique and language, the poem should belong to a later phase, but the presence of such motifs as the <u>fool</u> or the <u>clown</u> interwoven with the myth of Christ and the hospital world links it to previous poems I have already in this part of the book. The scene is set in a hospital where the patient is seeming having an encephalogram: doctors are again presented as judges, and the inmate is again guilty of having broken the rules of normality set up by society.

In the first stanza, Webb transposes the scene from the tribunal to the stage of a theater: hence the poet-clown-patient is now facing his audience of judge-doctors:

"A circus encephalograph
of grey silver-shiftless fog
Squirms for the audience and last erotic laugh,

Dances and dies before judicial headlight,
Before truth, falsehood - "

At the core of the poem is eventually the question of what is true and what is false in the reality of the hospital: the poet-patient-clown has to submit himself, his own life, his reality as a man, to the judgement of his doctors. But, as said previously, the doctors judge him from a false presupposition and false standpoint, in a falsified reality, where the rules set by society deny the freedom of "different" individuals - unless they are poets like Webb. In this case society is willing to accept their achievements, mystifying their significance and reducing the identity of the poet to a sort of fetish, thus turning the poet's reality into an alienated relationship, and the creation into objects to be adored on the altar of art.

The motif of the clown is brought forward by the final line of each stanza: from the reference to Pierrot in the first stanza, to that of Rice Dan, an American clown and showman who died in 1900. The identity of the doctors is again hinted at in the second stanza as:

"The robed aldermen and councillors with hangdog faces;
And doctors"

In the third stanza there is a shift of persona: the patient-clown is now addressed by the judge-doctors, while the clown has become the "Ego". This modification is indicative of Webb's awareness of his role as a "mentally-ill" person. His Ego, that is his consciousness, has to play the part of the clown on the stage of the hospital, the institution where doctors, like judges, represent and defend the values of the society of "normality". The function of the doctors is described indirectly by the lines,

".... we batten

> On shreds of your childhood
> Offered, pale simulacra, to our headlights."

The "circus-encephalograph", Webb's definition of the doctors' alienating role in relation to their patients, has in the third stanza further denotations by means of a series of oxymora: "our grudge and toy", "our distress" and "our joy". While in the final couplet "believes" rhymes with "grieves". The ambivalence of the judge-doctors' role, who toy with the identity of the patient-clown, is made clear in the last stanza, where the poet-patient-clown is replying to the judge-doctors:

> "Pull on your silver grey doughty
> Reappraisal of this man and this man"(p.175)

Here Webb's language is the key to his attitude towards the doctors' role: "doughty" carries all the humorous flavour of its archaic derivation. The reiteration of "man" in the second line undermines the seeming self-assurance conveyed by the demonstrative "this".

The last layer of meaning of the poem is laid bare in this stanza, where Webb refers to "a Cross", which is linked with a previous reference to "a Mass". In this way he foresees the role of the poet-patient-clown as that of the scapegoat-Christ, sacrificed on the altar-stage-court of the hospital-theater-tribunal. This role is turned from a negative one into a positive one thanks to the myth of Christ:

> "any clown of the troupe who has given
> .... receives, receives"

For the Christians/Catholics, sacrifice is never a meaningless feat: it always carries with it a cathartic message of redemption.

3.5 Myth of Christ and Sexual Imagery

"Beeston Regis"(p.289) re-proposes in a more elaborate language the interrelation between the myth of Christ and the sexual imagery. The poem begins with a series of impressionistic images juxtaposed together, which are reminiscent of the synesthesia at the beginning of "From the Cold". The opening stanza introduces the sexual theme in the line "Norfolk knew the tremor and shock of love", which is developed again in terms of opposites: "The firefly life in the huge palm of death", then in "Hauter studied at snowfall, humility", and before the end of the stanza, when the "he" and "she" of the poem are joined in the line "To have that final embrace and glitter at one with her", which introduces a long metaphor paraphrasing Christ's birth in the manger:

"While pedantic aeons nod like the three kings,
And pilgrim eternity stumbles in rags to earth...."

Christ's birth is associated with the beginning of life in the natural world by a series of anthropomorphic metaphora in the fourth stanza:

"The country is naked here,
His desire almost the living thought"(p.291)

"Cliffs roundabout muse upon pale prenatal
Anatomy in the jealous womb of ice"

The anthropomorphic metaphors serve as introduction to the personification of the Priory of Beeston Regis, which has "come into ruins" through a sort of destroying embrace with natural elements: "Has he gained her, held her fast?": Webb emphasizes this animistic intercorse with a chiasmus: "Lovingly, crumbled, O tumbled zealously". The sexual union is transfigured into a yearning for resurrection: "They are risen, they shall rise"(p.292), which is reiterated in the final couplet which works as a refrain:

"In the arising is the Calvary,
And the Beauty of the passing."

Webb's emphasis on the idea of sacrifice as a necessary step towards an illumination expresses the peculiar mysticism underlying *Socrates* as a whole. An indisputable mystical feature of his inspiration is the choice of sexual metaphors to characterize the union of the temporal and the eternal in the figure of Christ. Through the leit-motif reiterated by the refrain the poem focuses on the fixed moment in time through which man can have a glimpse of the eternal. The two lines closing the last stanza highlight this concept:

"Walls, mankind, yes, something of hungry earth
Melt into everlastingness, which is this hour."

The transposition of eternity in the moment in time is a further token of Webb's philosophical standpoint which, as said before, interprets reality in terms of immanence.

"Poet"(p.300) is the poem that best exemplifies Webb's identification with the myth of Christ. Here, as in "To a Doctor", Webb has a threaded through the structure a single metaphor based on the image of "a train of camels", which he broadens into a complex network of symbolic associations. The opening line of the poem defines the spatial dimension, a spiritual one: "I'm from the desert country". In a first section, the personality of the poet is literally equated with that of Christ; in a second section Webb differentiates himself from his persona and speaks both in first and second person, capitalized. It looks as if his personality is split into two halves, one identified with Christ and the other taking on the role of passive spectator.

By comparing Christ with a poet Webb redefines both his role and

Christ's: in the *Gospels* Christ is in a sense a poet, finding significance in everything he sees, and preferring a life of solitude and meditation. The central metaphor is developed on a first level through the "word" of the poet-Christ:

"So my lawless words (I speak figuratively)
Moved the desert, as a train of camels."

The other layer of connotations is related to the function of speech, which is "lawless"; Webb associated throughout the poem the word "law" with an assonance in "loam". This comparison has the function of externalizing the meaning of this association and its relation to the role of the Christ-poet, whose words are revolutionary, and as such opposed to the law of the masters and to their building-like connotation.

The second portion of the poem is written in anagogic language: Webb alludes to the account given in St John's Gospel of Christ and the woman taken in adultery. The kinship between Christ and the woman, who have both broken the law, is depicted by Webb, at first, through a familiar anthropomorphic metaphor:

"I have seen the sky at midnight
Bent earthward."(p.302)

Then, reshaping the central metaphor, "From the two together a train of camels." The sexual imagery develops at first the theme of love and is extended to the remaining connotations of the central metaphor. Webb implies by this process that real revolutionary words can be uttered only by the love springing from a union, be it sexual, be it of opposite forces. In the first stanza Webb has already hinted at this union in the metaphor,

"may words have edged their way obediently

Through the vast heat and that mythic cold of our evenings"

where the word "edge" suggests again the idea of suffering. The same connotations are expressed by "uneasy connubial whiteness". The poem ends with a revealing metaphor:

"The wind, as his delicate burning finger,
Gives a Word to the sand."

where the aridity of the sand is made fertile by the word of love, and by the wind, an image usually associated with the presence of God. Both are then connected through a simile to the strongly suggestive sexual image of the "burning finger" of Christ.

3.6 Synesthesia and the Use of Abstract Metaphors

"The Yellowhammer"(p.274) is highly reminiscent of "On First Hearing a Cuckoo", except that here the leit-motif is no longer based on the synesthetic combination of "green" and the cuckoo's sound: now Webb associates the song of the yellowhammer with "grey", a colour which was dominant in "October".

The first feature that draws the attention of the reader in this poem is the quality of metaphors, which is peculiar to this phase: "Age trickles", "the soused logos of the sun", "cloud-structures of reason crumble", "the ancient ritual brotherhood/Of light"(p.275). And further on we have, "Communiqué of the hammer-heart of God", "This is the grey rat nibbling at the soul",

the song, the footfall of the yellowhammer
Leaps of a sudden past the intellect,"

"Petty parables of the heretical will

Of power as conqueror."

and the more extended one,

> "... the steep groan, steel-blue claws of search
> And agony hither and thither scratched at earth,
> Frantic to clutch the centre and the form -
> Such fossicking could only end in death."

In particular, all the central images building up the metaphors: age, logos, reason, brotherhood, soul, God, intellect, will, power, search, agony, form, show a preoccupation with a different world of references from Webb's previous one. These metaphors have lost the sensual, almost tactile quality of their anthropomorphism and have come to embody more abstract relationships: they reach out from the senses to the mind and beyond in search of a spiritual dimension, from the merely physical they seek the metaphysical.

This tendency is also linked to the images concerning the externalization of the myth of Christ: in this poem, the image of the tree has the explicit function of introducing the presence of Christ, particularly by means of the reference to a "flagon of sap", a metonymy for the Eucharist. The tree symbolism, of which I already spoke in my analysis of "From the Cold", is then related to the "centre" and the "form" of the third stanza where it is linked by a reversed rhyme to the adjective/noun "true". While the metaphor "life cooked his supper zealously", with a somewhat manneristic touch, refers explicitly to Christ's Last Supper. The same metaphysical quality of the metaphors could be traced in all the poems belonging to this phase: in "Poet"(p.300) we have "a thousand warm humming stinging virtues", "mystical cold", "the wilful floating daze", my narrow clever desert eyes", and more extended,

"Many a star, the great lips of wonder drawn out, frozen,
Tempted me"

"... our horizon and the sky
Tremble together in uneasy connubial whiteness"

In "October"(p.346) the metaphors continue with "the famished sun all day", "Nibbles the stylus of our trivial good", "the silver grey occlusions of our distress", "the grey silver antics of our joy", and,

"the recalcitrant jacketed mighty
Countries howl"

But particularly in "Mousehold Heath"(p.348) we have a more powerful hints in "the night's helot traffics", "shrewish bungalow", "upon garbled trestles of memory", "Before time's skirt and shoulder", "innocent darkness", "objective gapings", "cautious neon", "such drugged effigies of good and evil must accomplish tomorrow", "So action and penalty are a leafless sleep", and the more extended one,

"Acres of freedom, vastness tremble at the notion
Of light treading with immortal rancours"

And the ending metaphors, which are linked more strictly to the myth of Christ:

"... in denial of past and future
Comes the patent of the moon above amice of cloud"

where the moon becomes part of the myth of Christ as in "Tell bread of the moon", "Fissures of love and agony, the unsounded maria", and another more extended metaphor,

"For this most ugly, old, distant, battered purity
Has past and future stumbling unsightly into light,

Heads bowed."

and again,

> "As nightshirted sin and value totter together
> Before the plate, the torn body"(p.355)

These excerpts, which could be multiplied if one looks at "Eyre All Alone", testify not only to the peculiar quality of the metaphors, but also and foremost to the indiscriminate redundancy of epithets, which have the disturbing function of dissolving the real and external world, in order to bring about a highly subjective representation of reality.

The comparative expansion of the metaphors through an overabundant use of qualifying epithets is a clear sign of Webb's intention to submerge the objectivity of the real in the infinite resonances of a plethora of personal, sentimental, fantastic and purely mental juxtaposition of experiences which stifles the life of the objects building up his metaphorical world. The manipulation and dissolution of the real in this phase is accompanied by a heightening of the religious inspiration of the poems, which accounts for Webb's gradual but not decisive escape into a private spiritual realm - the result of his subjectivism.

However, if one looks deeply at the syntactic structure of the poems, one comes to different conclusions: the poems are highly elaborated, and are no longer organized with a progressing and straightforward movement. To be sure, the semantic rendering of reality through syntax reveals Webb's modernity, as I have defined it previously: that is, he refrains from representing a reality devoid of its conflicts and inner tensions.

If we look back at "The Yellowhammer", here Webb begins with an inversion and a series of asyndetic present participles. The first stanza ends with a break into the linear semantic structure through the use of a future tense. The second stanza starts with an infinitive and another inversion in the first two lines, counterposed by the demonstrative "this", a sort of catalyst in the stanza. Then we have again a series of asyndetons and omissions of syntactic nexus which create a suspension in the composition of meaning, realizing a postponement of the communication of the overall meaning to the reader, who is indirectly called to participate in the compositional process of recreation of the poem's overall significance.

By this technique, Webb seems to affirm that meaning in life has to be recaptured bit by bit if one is to apprehend all the complexity of experience, as it is offered to the senses. The same lack of a uniform and linear pattern is detectable in the rhyme-scheme of these poems. The quantity of the lines in each stanza is no longer homogeneous: for instance, "The Yellowhammer" has a first stanza of 12 lines, a second of 13 lines, a third of 13 lines and a fourth of 11 lines. The same happens with "Poet" and "Mousehold Heath". Webb seems much more preoccupied with the creation of an internal syntactic and semantic structure, rather than of an external rhythmical pattern.

For instance, in the first stanza of "The Yellowhammer", we find quite a number of internal assonances and alliterations:

"docile lines of lands" / [s] and [l] repeated

"the soused logos of the sun
Lisps a last word from sallow wash and glimmer"/
    [s] and [l] and [w] repeated

These lines characterized by weak sounds like liquids, fricatives and approximants are used to introduce the contrasting central metaphor of the stanza:

"Cloud-structures of reason crumble without sound"/
[k][l] and [s][t][r] and [k][t] and [r] and [z]. then
again [k][r] and [b]]l] and [s] with a closing [n][d]

where the dominant sound is created by the presence of consonant clusters in which there is a clash between the profusion of liquid and sonorant phonemes combined with voiceless velar plosive: the metaphor contained in this line is, however, organized in such a way as to ease the tension expressed in the first half by presence of harsh consonant clusters, by slowly introducing in the word "reason" a sonorant with a voiced fricative and ending nasal, again a coupling of a voiced plosive with a liquid in "crumble", followed by a dental fricative in "without" and the final word combining fricative with a cluster of nasal+voiced plosive.

The same happens in the third stanza, where the alliteration between "steep" and "steal" made up by the combined effect of a harsh consonant cluster with two voiceless sounds [s][t], and the associated meaning, enhances the intensity of the metaphor and contributes a sense of obsession to the search.

At the same time, Webb does not shun semantic associations through the rhymes: in the second stanza "intersect" rhymes with "intellect", and "God" with "blood", and "brotherhood". In the third stanza, "search" rhymes with "march", "earth" and "death". It is also worth noting the introduction of a word like "fossicking", derived from colloquial Australian language used in goldmining. Its connection with the "centre" metaphor, which we already found in "The Canticle"(p.167), it at the opposite pole from an archaism like "pandering" used at the time.

The poem ends with the symbol of the tree, which has a reversed rhyme with "true", as I already remarked, and this second word rhymes with "blue", closing the poem. The word "blue" pertains to the creative side of personality and is opposed to "grey" denoting the informal. The importance of the tree symbolism in *Socrates*, acquires through this poem a further connotation: it expresses the idea of spiritual transformation. This is so particularly because the idea of rebirth and renewal, indissolubly linked to the seasonal transformation of the tree, is associated also in Jung's psychology with the image of the mother, which is physically lacking in Webb's life but is so important in Webb's psychic life.

As we shall see in the following chapter, the mother symbolism is ambivalent in that it can be understood both as a longing for spiritual rebirth but at the same time it can be interpreted as a regression into the self-destroying and deceiving security of the womb.

CHAPTER IV: THE STRUGGLE FOR SURVIVAL

4.1 The Artist as a Christ-Figure

In my analysis of *The Ghost of the Cock* I shall follow as faithfully as possible the original dating of the poems, that is I will start from "Around Costessey"(p.380) and particularly the central sections, which foreshadow the themes of "Poet" and "The Yellowhammer". I regard the whole of the sequence as a long poem on the artist as a Christ-figure, realizing his resurrection through the work of art. Webb explores this theme in relation to music in section 5, to painting in section 7, and in general to poetry. In the second poem "Our Lady's Birthday"(p.382), which follows a sort of historical introduction, are gathered all the basic clusters of images as to the redemption theme. In the first stanza Webb matches various semantic and symbolic fields by means of a polysyndeton, linking up a series of clauses by the conjunction "and". In this way he equates "a rippling" with "a tenderness" which is reiterated in order to bring forward its contrasting import in relation to "Calvary". "Tenderness" is also set in sharp focus by the parallel noun "guidance": both are counterpoised to "sunset".

The central metaphor of this poem is constituted by the idea of "birth" in the title, and is developed in the second stanza. Here birth is the result of the union of opposites forces: the "urchin sea" swallows up the sun, and in an explicitly sexual anthropomorphic metaphor "a tenderness coupling/White heat with goldenness". In the second stanza Webb transposes the moment of birth from the natural realm to the womb of the Immaculate: he concentrates on the mystery of Mary's pregnancy or the union of eternal - the Holy Spirit - with the temporal - the woman Mary. Pain and agony are inherent traits of this "spiritual" intercourse, which is referred to in the first line as Calvary and the redemption of mankind from the original sin, echoed in the last line as "lewd snake-bodied chasm"(p.201). The metaphor "the wicked chasm" in the final couples emphasizes the necessity to encompass even the dimension of sin in the movement towards redemption.

The quality of the metaphors is again typical of this phase: "Reservoirs of Heaven", "waters of the sun", "the seven/Rainbows sorrows", "womb of grace", "pedantic midwife earth", "a breast of value", "primitive sacred agony". Webb's poetic language is now shading the anagogic into the liturgical and the allegorical. Section 7 develops the previous themes in relation to painting: the opening line is a recurrent synesthetic association in Webb's work: "Bird-song is your reverberating touch"(p.390), where hearing, sight, and touch are all interfused together. The resurrection theme is developed on a network of metaphors: "metaphor is the enormous second frozen", which is broadened in "let my ungainly icicled pencil search/Down below zero", and the stanza ends with the word "risen".

In the third poem Webb says explicitly, "Your metaphor is this picture"(p.393), and further on "Metaphor and flesh await a resurrection"(p.393). In the hands of the artist words, colours, and nature become the means to "sign the posture of reality"(p.392), to bring from chaos to light the form, the essence, the "meaning of creation". Creation in the romantic conception of art, is made possible by the divine gift of inspiration: the legacy of the *vates* is to fulfil his vocation and resurrect through metaphor (and this is Webb's version) the form, the essence lying at the core of reality. In order to do so, he has to shape "a causeway between earth and heaven", "love" has to be linked with "pain" and the "merry grave", where "an outline of fullness" is "soberly embraced by shadow".

The language of this section is again peculiar to this phase:

"Your canny brush-stroke and beatitude
And hallowed second
....
I...genuflect
Before the mill and daring dated Cross"(p.391)

and always in the same page we find "Strangeness the womb of this alien prayerful place", "I rear my glass façade of metaphor", which is a sort of meta-metaphor. There is the same accumulation of epithets: "Serene genial currents of idling thunder", "the sinewy exquisite living winter flower", "the so tender voyaging line of truth", to quote only the more obvious. The sequence itself seems to lack a definite structure of themes and imagery: in the last poem Webb puts aside the main theme and introduces the image of an airman flying with his squadron, which he already explored at the end of "The Chalice", and which could only loosely be connected to his memories of the period passes at the R.A.A.F. in Canada.

Nonetheless, he mingles the theme of the flying airman with that of resurrection. At the beginning of the poem he focuses on Christ's passion on the cross; he introduces such liturgical words as "lector"(p.397) and "antiphon". Further on he broadens these references in the metaphors "the tiny Pilot nested, twisted upon his Cross", and "Conscience of the late tractor that straddled cloud,/Was hammed on nailhead". The closing line reaffirms the redeeming import of the myth of Christ: "Words of ploughed lands, of sunrise, and a Cross".

With "Song of Hunger"(p.401) Webb returns to the harmonious structures of some of the poems of *Socrates*. The central metaphor is based on the association of the sensation of hunger with the symbol of the Eucharist. Inside the poem, he builds a network of images and metaphors which are all pivoted on the central one: "To lick the mealy bowl of heaven dry"; "one cloud is loafing in my brain/As that fragrant unleavened bread"; "sacked larder", "Carbohydrate, sugar, fat, protein", "empty bowels", "one thousand calories", "mysteries of throbbing corn", and "surfeited with grace". By interlocking the two semantic and symbolic patterns the Eucharist brings life to the poet's self, whose condition is that of an ill man, as the references in the opening line clearly states. It is important to notice the peculiarities of the rhyme-scheme which is made of chained rhymes: in each stanza the C line is turned into the A of the following stanza, so that the sound-pattern of the poem is closely intervowen. The rhythm is pushed forward to the final single line which resolves the movement of the poem in the reiteration of the word "love", creating a suasive sound-effect.

The combination of these elements has led me to search for the psychological implications of the sexual symbolism: the union envisaged by the poet with the sun, of the "fiery Host"(p.402) of the Eucharist, is given peculiar sexual overtones in the final stanza, where the poet is looking for "your embrace"; the reference to "His tiny stall", or the stable where Christ was born, is then preceded by a metaphor, "rickety skeletal shanks work up above/Canvas", which calls to mind the canvas bed on which the poet is lying. The oral union of the Eucharist, the living bread, is then tied to the myth of Christ and to the symbol of the psychic child: the clue to this interpretation is also supplied by a longer metaphor in the second stanza of the poem:

"So the sacked larder of manhood hazards mice
Of memory, infant voices: foetal grain
Puts on a blossom's child-cajoleries;"

The child symbolism in this poem and in *The Ghost of the Cock* as a whole, is no longer the externalization of Webb's quest for a spiritual and psychic rebirth: it takes on a negative connotation and actualizes his yearning for a return into the maternal womb: in other words, it stands for regression and not for psychological progress. In this sense his quest for a personal myth can no longer be envisaged as a positive element in his psychic development. The child symbolism is also introduced in "On the Forgotten Artist"(p.415), where it is tied to the theme of the creative function of the artist, as in "Kookaburra on Television"(p.417) , and particularly in the last three poems I shall analyze, "On Going Free", "Nessun Dorma", and "Canobolas".

In this period of his life, Webb must have struggled hard for a psychic survival, as some of his poems clearly attest, particularly "Ward Two". Until after 1964, his conflicting interior world has overwhelmed the creative side of his psyche, with the collapse of his poetic activity. The long silence that follows is broken only by such liturgical - but notwithstanding beautiful - poems as "St Therese and the Child", or "Lament for St Maria Goretti", which reaffirm the persistence of the "child" and "mother" symbolism in its negative connotations.

At the same time, Webb is feeding his obsession with guilt and with sin, and he translates it into the acceptance of a vision of life and of reality to which pain and suffering - the equivalent of Christ's sacrifice on the Cross - are indissolubly linked. For instance, in "Derelict Church"(p.413), a typical liturgical and allegorical poem, we find "devouring sin and pain", and life paraphrased as "our debris" grating above the bones of the dead. The rationale behind this and his last poems is typically Catholic: life on earth is a continual struggle against the temptations of the flesh, and is only functional to the life of the spirit after death.

4.2 The Ward and the Poet-Patient-Fool

"Ward Two"(p.418) is certainly the more conspicuous achievement of this book, which is not one of his best in my opinion.

Webb himself admitted this fact in a conversation with Dr Craig Powell: "It was a horrible mess - scraps of note paper ... - I tied it all in a bundle and sent it to Angus and Robertson ... Somehow they organized it into a book and they brought it our as "The Ghost of the Cock"(p.434). In this sequence Webb focuses again on the figure of the poet-patient-fool we already met previously and which is here explored with a wider scope and breadth.

The introductory poem "Pneumo-encephalograph"(p.418) depicts the figure of the artist who has to undergo pain in order to bring to light, or to beget and give birth to, his poetic creation: "Of pain's amalgam with gold let some man sing" says Webb, and the inversion is asymptomatic of his concern with pain. This poem, like most of Webb's work, is obviously highly autobiographical. The dimension of pain is evidenced by a juxtaposition of opposite images: the metaphor "flints coupling for the spark" conveys both the idea of pain and the necessity to match together opposite forces in order to give birth to the poetic creation. The same applies to "Passion and peace trussed together", and the chiastic oxymoron "Hour stalking lame hour", to the combination of "bone and vessel", connected again to the ideal of "coupling". With this series of tropes Webb combines such metaphors as "supple as the flute"(p.419), "mouths that are almost mute", or the compound "improbable will", echoing the metaphor at the beginning of the poem "Today's guilt and tomorrow's blent" which rhymes with "impotent".

His intention if that of giving an intimation of the uncertainty involved in the process of creation, a sense of something impending which is not dependent on the will of the poet, but on some external power, a suspension which dramatizes the action of the poet. Furthermore, the reference to "guilt" and the presence of the "Holy Spirit" at the end of the poem serve as an introduction to the Christ's mythical dimension. With "Harry"(p.420) Webb enters into a definite time and spatial dimension: the hospital. His concern now is not merely with the poet, as a separate entity epitomizing the condition of all the inmates; through his persona he is now everyman, and the inmate writing a letter becomes the epitome for the condition of man imprisoned in the four walls of the hospital's room. Webb depicts the life in the ward in a painfully realistic way: Harry lives "Among walls of the no-man's land"(p.421); he wears "the striped institutional shirt", and writes with an "institutional pen".

Webb's lucid and clear-cut attack against the hospital, as an institution equated with the prison, is externalized in the lines:

"Because the wise world has for ever and ever rejected
Him and because your children would scream at the sight
Of his mongol mouth stained with food...."

Here nothing more is left to the imagination: Webb's awareness of the stigma set on different people like him by society is uttered in explicit and unambiguous terms. "We have been plucked from the world of commonsense" is his explicit accusation, and Harry is the real "moron", a "pudgy Christ", his mind an "altar-stone". Webb's ironic self-awareness is not only attested by the detachment through his persona: it is also expressed explicitly in the lines:

"An imbecile makes his confession,
Is filled with the Word unwritten, has almost genuflected."

But self-consciousness is accompanied by the patent complicity with the inmate-fool: "he has resurrected/The spontaneous through retarded and infantile Light"; "Transfigured with him we stand"; a complicity which is not devoid of compassion: "He writes to the woman, this lad who will never marry".

4.3 The Ward as a Prison

In "Old Timer"(p.422) Webb develops the same theme, again in explicit terms: the figurative "virus" in the first line, "Eating its way.../In a multitude of cozening wheedling voices", is sucking and devouring the "Being" of the inmate-poet-fool, who is depicted as something "tender and succulent and porous": the hospital has become the prison-like institution where man is despoiled of his being, of his identity. The "four paternal walls of stone" are equated to the "Gauleiters", the Nazi district: Webb no longer depicts the hospital as an innocuous church, as was the case with the poems in *Socrates*. Now it is as a concentration-camp where the "mentally ill" individual becomes the "Enemy":

"Isolate the Identity, clasp its dwindling head.
Your birth was again the birth of the All,
The Enemy..."

Webb is here extending the metaphor of the inmate-poet-fool in "Pneumo-Encephalograph" taking on the role of the enemy, "Contraband enters your brain/Puckered guerrilla faces patrol the vein"(p.419), resumed in "Harry" with the words "loot", "shards we could steal", and the longer reference,

"He has purloined paper, he has begged and cadged
The bent institutional pen"(p.420)

The inmate-poet-fool-prisoner is envisaged as the Enemy in the prison-concentration-camp of the hospital, the institution created by the society of doctors and normal people in order to rob and destroy the different identity of the inmate[31].

---

[31] It has been the Law 180, introduced in Italy in 1978 by the work of a famous psychiatrist and named after his

Webb is painstakingly aware of his impotence to rescue his identity, so that even the poetic creation becomes a fictitious substitute:

"To guard your spark borrow the jungle art
Of this hospital yard, stamp calico vestures
For H.M. Government, for your funeral"(p.422)

and further on,

"So we become daily more noncommittal
This small grey mendicant man must lean
Against his block of wall, old eyes rehearsing time
Whose hanged face he is."(p.423)

Even the pantomime of the inmate-poet-fool-prisoner's everyday life is defined with direct and unambiguous terms:

"I take my fatal vital
Steps to the meal, the toilet"(p.423)

or is reflected in the asyndetic and tragic conciseness of the line,

"Sit, feed, sleep, have done."(p.422).

The fourth poem of the sequence, "Ward Two and the Kookaburra" (p.423), is a sort of mythological interval, which leads the reader into Webb's symbolic and metaphoric inner world. Thus the world becomes the World, the walls the Wall, and the yard the Yard, all capitalized; we are taken into the night and through "sleep's non-magnetic field"(p.424) with a series of anthropomorphic and expressionist metaphors, creating a sort of animistic background where the poet's deterministic and fatalistic view of life is laid bare:

---

surname "Legge Basaglia", that started the closing of all the asylums and its substitution by controlled houses where the mentally ill inmates where left free to go in and out.

"... snap of the thick thumb
From somewhere, and the moon with the lined face,
Old voyageuse, dined on her continental crumb,
And sea-sauce...."

The mysterious agent coming from "somewhere" is embodied by the kookaburra, described as a "lumbering giant ghost of laughter", whose "guffaw" turns the persona's "belief" into "grief". The ironic attitude of the poet is confirmed by a bitter realization of impotence, "Gape at your porridge, munch it like a god!", where "god" might easily be turned into "dog".

The next poem, "Homosexual"(p.425) takes us definitely from the exterior world, where the inmate-poet-fool-prisoner is related to his society, into the interior world, where he has to related himself to his being, to his identity. Here everything is looked at from the inside out: the poem starts with the image of an inner eye reifying the personality of the persona. "To watch may be deadly.../And the object becomes ourselves. That is the terror"; the action of "watching" could lead to the realization of the state of complete alienation, in which he is living, and of which he is nonetheless aware: "We have simply ceased, are not dead, and have been/And are."

But the awareness of an object-like existence leads the poet to account for his and for those human beings' difference, for their living in a place where their "movement is relegated", and their thought and being "are given over", as Webb himself puts it:

"So, at this man's ending, which is all a watching,
Let us disentangle the disgust and indifference,"

And in the following stanza he describes the process through which alienation, reification and "schizophrenia" are brought about: the two personal subjects "I" and "He" become the interior agent and audience to the split inside the inmate-poet-fool-prisoner: the "He" is the side of the personality which is different, ill, abnormal, deviated, alienated, reified, which is born inside and grows "unselfconscious as the loveliest of flowers"(p.426).

The someone is made to enter his psyche, and "Pale glass faces contorted in hate or merriment/Embody him": this highly suggestive metaphor is the leit-motif of the poem. The "faces" that want to "embody" the inmate-poet-fool-prisoner are the faces of normal people in the society of normality, wanting to give him a "normal" body, in accordance with the rules and the codes of society. But,

"... Something nameless as yet
Resists embodiment. Something, the perennial rebel,
Will not rest..."

It is this something, which determines his deviation, his diversity from the norm, that "becomes his terror". Thus the persona is torn between two opposite poles: on the one side, he is aware of his deviation from the codes of society; on the other, this realization brings an element of terror in his self, terror of being the rebel, of being different - even though he has been given the divine spark of inspiration - and of belonging to a group of people relegated in the ghettoes of mental hospitals because of their deviance.

Hence the terror of "watching" inside, hence the awakening in his conscience of the feeling of "sin beginning, our sin", a feeling against which it is impossible to fight. But which is passively accepted as it is accepted the fact of being part of a "schizophrenogenic" society, that is a society that causes and generates schizophrenia in the mentally weak or mentally inherited condition of some individual. This is why the acceptance of sin is not dissociated from the acceptance of the difference:

"He will differ, must differ among all the pale glass faces,
The single face contorted in hate or merriment."

The following stanza described the realization by the parents of the difference of their son:

"he is mulcted of words, remain to him only
The words of sin, escape, which is becoming all of life."

Sin becomes "flesh, the concrete, the demanded", it is what the exterior world charges him with, and is part of him like his difference, his illness, as Webb puts it:

"But all his compatriots in sin or in other illness
Are flesh, the demanded, silent, watching, not hearing:
It is all he ever sought." (p.427)

To be part of the community of different people becomes a privilege, a mystical illumination: "I am tempted to say he has found God", says Webb; or "He is loving us now, he is loving all", and the hospital becomes the place of miracles, its walls become "unambiguous". The interlude "A Man"(p.428) creates a sort of nightmarish atmosphere in the sequence: the persona is a man who can "hardly walk", "wrestling with consonants"; he is

"like a king behind a heavy lock,
Niched in and almost part of solid wall".

The scenery is completed by

"Canaries silent and spiders, caged in laws,
... begging a First Cause
That they may tear It open with their claws"

and by a "goldfish", "weeds", and "old cunning fox" and a "redbronze gadfly". The poem has a haunting rhythm created by the reiteration of the word "wall" and by the rather gloomy refrain at the end of each stanza; images overlap in a sort of montage, or as a sequence of old shots in an album. There is, however, one image which is resumed in the next poem, and is the image of the Cup, the "King's Cup"(p.429). In "The Old Women"(p.430) the hospital is the place that "holds the fugitive vessel to be kissed": the motif of the vessel, the cup of the king, is reminiscent of the Holy Grail, a feminine symbol, holding Christ's blood - a motif we already found in "The Chalice". The final poem of the sequence is dedicated to a blonde girl, who in a sense is an embodiment of this symbol, and who concludes seemingly the quest.

The poem "The Old Women" reproposes the theme of "A Death at Winson Green": the visitor entering the ward from the exterior world. But this time the hospital is not only placed in a mythical scenery, it becomes a completely different planet lost in a foreign galaxy. The poem is characterized by its astronomical language: "Son, husband, lover, have spun out of orbit"; "Men like meteorites enter their atmosphere"; "Gravity bends to an earlier law in this place". The ward is lost not only in space, but also in a prehistoric "Ice Age of the cherished calculated fear"(p.430), where the final oxymoron repeats the basic metaphor of "Homosexual".

However, one cannot help noticing that the sequence has progressively lost its cogency and directness: most of the themes proposed and developed in the previous poems have lost their grip, if they have not been abandoned at all. "Ward Two" constitutes Webb's last attempt at a harmonic longer poem, partly failed; the radio play "The Ghost of the Cock" is better organized, but is written in a kind of religious-allegorical language. One has obviously to take into account the span of time intervening between the publication of the body of

"Ward Two" and that of the final poem of the sequence, "Wild Honey".

Even so, it is hard to find a connection whatsoever among their themes, imagery, and language. Webb reintroduces "grey" in this poem, and associates it with the image of the "rain", which has a sort of cathartic function. Greyness will gradually be substituted by the "golden" colour of the girl's hair, who is an embodiment of spring. The figure of the girl is associated with the idea of purity and innocence:

"... and see, stranger,
The overcoated concierge of death
As a toy for her gesture"(p.434)

says Webb, and seems to foreshadow a return to an edenic state, beyond the dimension of time, notwithstanding the Fall:

"....see faith
As all such essential gestures unforbidden,
Persisting through Fall"

This prefiguration is projected in a realm completely foreign to the reality set in prospect by the sequence as a whole: it is dictated by Webb's escapism, or by his realization of impotence in coming to grips with his real problems.

The apocalyptic reunion of all creatures at the end of "The Ghost of the Cock"(p.434) is also transposed into a mythico-allegorical realm, at the end of time. The whole play envisages, as a solution to the problem of everyday life, an escape from the historical reality into a mythical one. Webb no longer wishes to have the two realities interact with one another, and bring about a new one, where society and the individual are no longer a duality but are dialectically related. He has definitely taken shelter in the mother's womb, he has accepted his condition as "paranoid schizophrenic".

4.4 The Mother and the Return into the Womb

The last remarkable poems written by Webb are all centered on anthropomorphic representations of the mother symbol: the earth, the hill or the mountain are turned into the mother's breast. "Canobolas"(p.376) has been discussed by A.D.Hope in Poetry Australia [32], as to its mythic and symbolic associations; but Hope restricts his comments to these symbolic patterns inside the poem and does not enter into the metaphysical and psychological meaning of the imagery. This is why he omits to comment on the last two stanzas of the poem. The poem is balanced between life and death, light and darkness, day and night; Christ is again the mediator, and as such he embodies and reconciles the two opposing forces, as the mother symbol does.

The mother is also a giver of life, hence a symbol of rebirth like Christ. But, as said previously, the symbol of the mother is ambivalent: Webb concentrates on this ambivalence, rather than on the analogy with Christ. The mother symbol is given a metaphysical meaning by her embodiments: she becomes the mediator between earth and sky, time and eternity. Eventually it symbolizes Webb's "grave Wish" for the life of the spirit.

The final word of the third stanza, "devotion", gives a clear religious tone to the spiritual search; while "sink" resumes the association of the mother symbolism with the ocean, into which the sun-Christ is plunging, as "an ancient broad-mouthed comprehensive one in the last stanza, where the reader is addressed in metaphorical terms: "learn from her true Form and be wise", the Form of being "a gentle concave", the mother's eyes full of "darkness" and the earth having to "muzzle her tender swell" as children do. Webb's invitation is for a

---

[32] A.D.Hope,"Talking to God - The Poetry of Francis Webb", *Poetry Australia cit.*, pp.31-35

return to the false security of the womb, where one "sinks" into "darkness" and obliteration: in the opening line, Webb's "Wish" is a "grave" wish, a lethal wish for death and nor for life.

The same symbolic associations can be detected in "On Going Free"(p.460), in more explicit terms. In the first stanza a series of negations are accumulated: "negative electron", "uncharged hills and buses", "anger", "malnourished flowers are not alive", "Nor is light light nor is green green, "hunger", "inertia", which are all converging towards the "nucleus", the "pivot", searching for "grace", "that is yourself". In the following stanza an intimation of the "Other" is materialized, and this presence is meant to give meaning and life, hence to affirm the series of negations of the first stanza. This being is again a personification of the mountain, Canobolas, into a mother symbol, from which stems the "child", the psychic child.

"I stood and begged my homing, and there grew
The Child….
Frowning me on my way and on to you."

The return to the womb is envisaged in animistic and sexual terms: "the lewd hill" is turned into a womb-vagina, and "to its fleshless shoulder clung a tree"(p.461). In the last stanza, Webb introduces a shift in the process of personification: the tree embodies the poet who is speaking in first person:

"I cannot know what …
… whimsical impetus fixed my sheer absurd
Shoulders around your disoriented root"

And "My slackened shoulder-blades creaked whenever you stirred". The reference to the cross at the end of the third stanza and the metaphor: "You bore the spirit in your branches like a bird", hint at the identification of the tree with the cross and with the poet-Christ. But their association with the mother-mountain evidences the condition of the poet, with its roots in the womb of the hospital-prison, which like the earth is becoming his grave. Imprisoned as he is in his womb-like condition, his only freedom is a flight, in the spirit, to heaven, like a bird.

"Nessun Dorma"(p.461) might be regarded as Webb's testament, both creatively as a poet, and psychologically as a human being. In the first stanza he elaborated the same symbolic network of associations we found in "Canobolas": light and dark, night and day, life and death are interwoven. He also takes up some of his early material in the metaphor:

"... the night
Will be all an abyss and depth of light between
Two shorelines in labour: birth and death."

The coincidence of the opposites is matched by two further associations: a religious one in "O passion/(One light is the hospital window) of quickening light", which hints at his condition in the asylum; and a psychological-spiritual one, "O foetus quaking towards light". The second stanza is dominated by the word "death" reiterated in the third and the last line, and echoed by the movement of the images progressing towards night and darkness. These opaque internal associations are further elaborated in the metaphors "harrowed palms of the sill"(p.247), "lacerate my paling cheeklines", "tears, flood me". Pain and water are thus merged with death and darkness.

The symbol of the child appears in the metaphor "the dawning child" and in the final lines of the poem which paraphrase an ambiguously purifying death:

"Till the cry of the infant emergent, lost and lame,

Is the cry of a death gone towering towards the Flame."

The image of the flame, capitalized, points to the symbolic realm of the spirit, which is Webb's yearning; but to attain it man has to go through a double death: as a human being returning to the womb; and through the symbolic death of the psychic child. The "infant" is depicted "lost and lame", which rhymes with "Flame". In this semantic association Webb indicated his belief in the necessity to undergo an ulterior process of suffering and pain, after the psychological rebirth intimated by the child symbol, if one has to attain a true spiritual rebirth. The conclusion to which the poem leads is that one cannot escape guilt and sin, a precondition based on religion which has as its foundation sin and guilt like the Catholic religion and its "original sin".

Only by establishing these foundations, which enslave the spiritual life of man to a view of life made of suffering and pain, will redemption and resurrection lose their parentage with death.

4.5 A Short Introduction to Chapter V and VI

As discussed in section 1.6 above, words in Webb's poetry and in general in all poetry are very important. Words' meaning is even more important. In addition, poetic devices may impose specific choices in order to match the line in which words are contained, the stanza and what's more the rhyme or the poetic device that the poet has in mind to realize. This is why a chapter on quantitative features of word-forms is important, which highlights Webb's peculiar and almost maniacal search for specific word-forms in every context and makes his vocabulary so rich that it compares with the richest ever amongst contemporary poets. Besides looking for word-forms specialties the chapter based on computation focuses on meaning by concentrating on the semantics, but also on abstract properties and structural syntactic features. Thus the two chapters combined give a full picture of the poetic language used by Webb.

CHAPTER V: A QUANTITATIVE ANALYSIS OF LINGUISTIC DEVIATION

5.1. Signs and Sense

When talking about art, people tend to confuse genius and madness, poetic imagination and creative inspiration in the personality of the great artist. However, when criticizing an artist, or when expressing professional judgements of some sort, people tend to dissociate the two entities, man and the artist.

While talking about Webb to the Head of Melbourne Mental Hospital, Webb's poetry had been defined as a token of schizophrenic language; obviously, the same didn't apply to people living in the opposite world, the world outside the hospital, who disregarded the fact that Webb was mentally ill and regarded and still regard his poetry as the work of a highly creative mind. The two entities, man and the poet coexist only thanks to a convention: in both cases, the rules of society set the two worlds - the mentally normal and the mentally abnormal - previously euphemistically joined, irreconcilably and widely apart.

This is due to the rules of a society which is unable or unwilling to cope with such abnormalities as those constituting mental illness.

Indeed, a psychiatrist is hardly willing to account for the fact that a person, labeled "paranoid schizophrenic" might be a great poet too; besides, the literary society is strongly unwilling to accept mental illness as a component of the muse, or of the creative source of inspiration.

People tend, however, to confuse and consequently to misjudge mental abnormalities. Generally speaking, mental disorders can be mapped on two distinct areas:

- mental handicaps, which are mental disorders including such cases as people born mentally "subnormal", deficient, retarded, backward or even idiots. These people are born mentally handicapped, that is, they have a brain damage, a lack of brain development and so on, and cannot be "cured" or treated. Deficiencies and causes are well-known in this case;
- mental illness, which affects people who started out by being normal, have a mental illness and in some cases may become normal again. One becomes mentally ill, and is not born with it. No one knows what causes mental illness - the aethiology of the illness, how can someone be fruitfully and completely cured?

There are many closely-linked issues that go to build up the image of the mentally ill: our world is at the heart a world of multifactorial problems and no simple solution can really easily be put forward. The most quoted reasons for mental illness remain always two: stress placed on the individual by the urban society, highly competitive, a factor which contributes to increase vulnerability to such mental damage, the more so for people who are psychologically vulnerable or have inherited such characteristic as part of their personality.

Moreover, there is a form of social deprivation due to the fact that we live crammed together yet in isolation, a conflicting reality that contributes a feeling of alienation instead of belonging.

Besides, normality like health is not a firmly definable state: no one is always perfectly healthy both physically and mentally. There are ups and downs day by day. Mental health is thus an ill defined state: we all live our lives in states spanning normality and abnormality. "Normal" people have feelings of anxiety and depression. Some people may move back and forth into the area of mental illness, some of them get to the point of taking their own life as a result of that state.

When we say that someone is abnormal, perhaps, it is because certain behaviour frightens us and we gain comfort by classifying him/her into a category. If then, normal equals acceptable, we need to acknowledge the fact that there are degrees of acceptability varying with time and social status.

Is it not perhaps the fear of mining the foundation itself of social status and of social acceptability that prevents people from conceiving as equally acceptable people who are unable or unwilling to adapt and to coexist without conflicts with the rest of the society?

5.2 Semiotics and feedback devices

In that perspective, normality becomes the acquisition of a set of controlling abilities over the process of coding and decoding the sign system of a society at a given temporal span. The information content of messages delivered by the media, seen as an arm of the acquisitive society, gets a lot of blame for creating dissatisfaction, too. People who are unable to develop one's own built-in and properly controlled feedback device for an adequate defense of their status in all kinds of social intercourse, become outcasts. And for a man like Webb, secluded in mental hospitals for most of his life, no real feedback had been allowed.

The mentally ill are thus compelled or rather condemned into a state of linguistic and physical alienation which is the worst kind of social deprivation ever conceived by a human mind.

As long as an individual stays a member of "normal" society he is allowed a degree of abnormality, according to the degrees of acceptability determined by current conventional rules, by the social group he belongs to, etc. Whenever the individual resorts to some kind of impatience or intolerance towards the social environment he is in danger of being labeled as mental ill to be "cured". The "cure" becomes synonymous with a social selecting device, automatically switched on whenever an individual is reputed harmful - both physically and ideologically speaking - or simply an hindrance, an impediment for his community.

What kind of deviation causes society to reject people as abnormal? Or is it a question of degree of deviation that matters?

Society accepts to a certain degree levels of eccentricity, personal idiosyncrasies, unconventional or nonconformist behaviour expressed both linguistically and/or by bodily attitudes and gestures. Here again there are rules and degrees that define the threshold level of acceptability allowed to the individual, which is usually determined by the social group he belong to. If someone breaks a shop window today he would probably be taken to police and made to reimburse the shop owner. At Webb's times, in the '60s, he would be taken as he was taken, into a mental hospital.

Linguistically speaking, normality is a well-defined level of control of the rules of the communicative situation. These rules can only be violated according to a set of conditions related to some variables present in a given situation. Each one must know these conditions and the presence of some random variable, he must accept and conform to there rules to be communicative: in other words, he has no possibility to manipulate the codes and modalities of speech intercourses on a social level.

How many times people think the opposite of what they say: this gap is a kind of linguistic alienation which each member of a social community suffers as long as he is not the one that possesses the levers of power.

5.3 Poetry as deviation from the norm

Poetry is a form of linguistic behaviour that deviates from the norm and that breaks the rules set up by the code established by society, which is tolerant, accepted and even extolled. In fact, poetic creation is regarded as the highest form of symbolic activity of the human mind, a real act of civilization, indeed.

Linguistic norm is thus violated systematically and theories have been built upon this deviation like Brecht's *Entfremdung* and Shklovskij's *Ostranenie*. Contemporary poetry has come to the point of building up a sort of anti-language as a means to express linguistic alienation. It is a language deprived of the usual connotations - the meaning attached to symbols - of the usual denotation - the meaning attached to the signs - and of the usual referents - the objects related to the signs.

Poetry means in that it is the expression of social pathologies and is nonetheless accepted as an anti-formal message. The status of poetry and of other artistic contemporary expressions like painting, is thus intrinsically ambiguous, deviating and intentionally abnormal; but its acceptability is warranted by its being a code endowed with an aesthetic function. The rules are thus reverted: the elements of expression must be new, unforeseeable, unpredictable, at the antipodes of the communicative function of linguistic praxis in usual everyday social intercourse. The aim of the artist is that to stun the reader/visitor in order to help release her/his imagination from the fetters imposed by common coding-decoding linguistic/visual processes.

Language has to work on a semantic level much more than on a syntactic one; it has got to possess a high degree of entropy, because it must work on paradigmatic or associative links rather than on syntagmatic or contiguity ones - even though metaphors are elaborated on a linear contiguous level between two or more syntactically related words.

In this case we may say that deviation equals creativity when the linguistic code is "misused" with an aesthetic function: Francis Webb's poetry not only deviates as such from the linguistic form, but it would also deviate from the aesthetic norm if there were a fixed one. Its lexis and its use of metaphors is indisputably an example of how rich the creative imagination can be.

In order to show that in quantitative terms I have organized a separate chapter which encompasses all the studies I have previously published which include comparisons with most important contemporary English and American poets, and also a comparison with W.B.Yeats whole work and with the American Norm, as recorded in the Brown Corpus edited by Kucera and Francis.

5.4 Quantitative Lexical Comparison with W.B.Yeats and American Norm

Yeats' lexis or poetic canon comprises 138,485 occurrences or tokens and a number of 10,666 types, or different unique individual words. Webb's corpus comprises 63,238 tokens and 11,600 types, that is less than half the number of tokens with about thousand types more than Yeats. Webb's vocabulary richness (VR) or mean frequency is very low $(64,238/11,000) = 5.45$ if compared to Yeats $(138,485/10,666) = 12.33$ and to the American Norm, $(1,014,000/50,406) = 20.12$ where the figures between parenthesis are respectively the tokens total divided by the types total. Another measure of Vocabulary Richness is given by the so-called Repetition Rate, which can be derived by subtracting from the unity, the Ratio of Hapax, where Hapax indicate how may words have been used only once referred obviously on the Types total which is for Webb very high, (6667/11600) = 0,57, meaning that over fifty percent of types are hapax legomena; whereas for Yeats we get (4698/10666) = 0,44.

Thus the Repetition Rate(RR) for Webb is 1-0,57=0,43, whereas for Yeats 1-0,44=0,56 indicating how strikingly apart the two corpora are. A RR so low - below 0.50 - does not allow us to apply the Herdan-Waring distribution law.

We can no doubt affirm that Webb's vocabulary has a very deviant word distribution, which as we shall check statistically further on, is highly significant. In fact, we can say that Webb's vocabulary word distribution does not obey any particular law, since there is no correspondence nor any agreement whatsoever between the expected distribution and the actual one.

To test the lexical distinctive features of the poets we collected all Q-words in the two corpora to show how peculiar the lexicon of Webb's poetry is.

Table 1. *Q-words total figures in Webb and Yeats*

	Yeats	Webb
TYPES	42	56
TOKENS	138	110
\=TYPES	15	30
\=TOKENS	31	46

where the sign \= indicates the difference of types and/or tokens used by the two poets: Yeats used 15 types with 31 tokens different from Webb, whereas Webb used 30 types with 46 tokens different from Yeats. This difference is to be interpreted as a further sign of Webb's lexical richness.

To check lexical similarities and dissimilarities we prepared a list reported below in Table 2. which emphasizes words peculiar to the one or the other poet. We decided to limit ourselves to examine the rank list down to the hundredth lexical entry approximately and reported them both separately and in comparison.

Table 2. *List of lexemes belonging to the three rank lists examined individually or in their combination*

N.	Yeats	Webb	Webb/Yeats	Webb/A.N.	Yeats/A.N.
1	Heart	Face	Light	Last	Made
2	Sang	Death	Old	Good	Great
3	Cried	Earth	Wind	Life	Found
4	Bleed	Green	Dead		Night
5	Moon	Air	Love		Give
6	Song	Grey	God		Take

7	Young	Voice	Stone		Years
8	Stood	Blue	Live		Seemed
9	Soul	Hitler	Star		
10	Mind	Darkness	Tree		
11	Bring	Past	Dreams		
12	King	Colour	Die		
13	Hair	Peace	Sun		
14	Body	Cold	Sea		
15	Wandering	Doctor	Bird		
16	White	New	Child		
17	Lady	Yellow	Let		
18		Dark			
19		Pain			
20		Shadow			
21		Hour			
22		Brain			
23		Silver			

Webb and Yeats share 36 lexemes, but Webb's list appears the most peculiar one sharing only three lexemes with A.N. Even though this comparison is limited to the most frequent words in each corpus the difference with A.N. is striking, as is the agreement between the two poets. We looked into Montale's - the most famous contemporary Italian poet - word list and found a lot of similarities again limiting ourselves to the most frequent words. Here is the list of the first 34 lexemes with a translation for every Italian word, listed according to their rank.

Table 3. *List of words in Montale's highest rank and their translation*

VITA-life, MANO-hand, MONDO-world,
SAPERE-know, TEMPO-time, SERA-evening,
GIORNO-day, LUNGO-long, TERRA-earth,
LUCE-light, VEDERE-see, ALBERO-tree,
MARE-sea, VENTO.wind, DISCENDERE-descend,
OMBRA-shadow, VOLO-flight, MEMORIA-memory,
CIELO-sky, FARE-make, SOLO-alone,
VOCE-voice, FONDO-bottom, SUONO-sound,
CUORE-heart, PORTARE-take, FUOCO-fire,
SOLE-sun, UOMO.man, GIUNGERE-arrive,
ACQUA-water, ALTO-high, PASSARE-pass
ARIA-air,

A simple comparison with Webb and Yeats shows the marked differences and similarities:

- Webb/Yeats: light, wind, life, tree, sun, sea, (6 over 17)
- Webb: earth, man, know, see, day, water, air, long, past, shadow (10 over 23)
- Yeats: heart, bring,
- A.N.: make, life,

So it seems that Montale shares a lot with Webb's imagery when compared to Yeats, who eventually belonged to a previous century. Here below in Table 3. we report the list of all Q-types found in Webb and Yeats poetry, with their frequency in parenthesis.

Table 4. *Lexical Comparison between Yeats and Webb based on Q-Words*

	WEBB	YEATS
1.	(1) QUACKSILVERING	QUARRIED
2.	QUALMS	QUARRY
3.	QUANDARY	QUATRAINS
4.	QUANTUM	QUAY
5.	QUARRIED	QUENCHED
6.	QUARRYING	QUERN
7.	QUARTERED	QUESTIONS
8.	QUARTZ	QUESTS
9.	QUAVERING	QUICKLIME
10.	QUE	QUICK-LIME
11.	QUEERLY	QUIET-EYED
12.	QUEER-SHAPED	QUIET'S
13.	QUEST	QUINTO-CENTO
14.	QUI	QUIRE
15.	QUICKEN	QUIRES
16.	QUICKENINGS	QUITE
17.	QUICKENS	QUOTE
18.	QUICKSANDS (2)	QUAFFED
19.	QUICKSILVER	QUATTRO-CENTO
20.	QUIETER	QUEEN-WOMAN
21.	QUIETEST	QUEER
22.	QUILLS	QUENCH
23.	QUILL'S	QUICK
24.	QUILT	(3) QUAKING

25.	QUIP	QUATTROCENTO
26.	QUITS	QUENCHLESS
27.	QUITTED	QUESTIONER
28.	QUIVERED	QUICKLY
29.	QUOTA	QUIETNESS
30.	QUOTED	QUIETUDE
31.	QUOTES	QUIVER
32.	(2) QUANTITY	(4)QUARRELS
33.	QUARTER-HOUR	QUESTIONING
34.	QUEEN	(5)QUALITY
35.	QUEENS	QUARREL
36.	QUENCH	QUARRELING
37.	QUERULOUS	QUESTIONED
38.	QUESTIONED	(6) QUARTER
39.	QUESTIONING	QUEST
40.	QUIETNESS	(11) QUEENS
41.	QUIXOTE	QUESTION
42.	QUOTE	QUIVERING
43.	(3) QUAKE	(12) QUICKEN
44.	QUAKES	
45.	QUAKING	
46.	QUARREL	
47.	QUARRY	
48.	QUEASY	
49.	QUIVERING	
50.	(4) QUAINT	
51.	QUICKENINGS	

52.   (5) QUARTERS
53.   QUESTIONS
54.   QUICK
55.   (6) QUIETLY
56   (7) QUEER

Webb has a higher number of Q-types - around 150, but Yeats has a higher number of Q.tokens more than 170.

5.5 A comparative quantitative analysis of Vocabulary Richness

One of the most valuable element in the evaluation of a poet careful treatment of meaning and words derives from the analysis of the socalled Vocabulary Richness – also referred to as Type-Token Ratio. This is derived from the ratio computed on the basis of Types and Tokens. Tokens are the total number of words considered, in this case all the words used by Webb as documented in his Collected Poems, in their actual number of occurrences, single or repeated. Types are those same words but taken only once. Words are in this case corresponding to wordforms and not to lemmata, that is there are still types that duplicate the same lemmata in the case of nouns, because they include both singular and plural forms, if existent in the frequency count. As for verbs, there are usually 4 different forms for regular verbs and there may be up to 6 different wordforms for the same lemma. To compute Vocabulary Richness (hence VR) one needs then two quantities: total number words or tokens, after erasing punctuation; total number of types that is tokens taken only once.

I did this for a number of different poets and for a number of corpora available which contain non poetic writing, this in order to get a baseline for comparison. Of course we expect there to be a great difference between the two realms: normal prose writing should have a much lower value than poetry. It is also important to note that the Type/Token Ratio alone by itself is not a good indicator of VR. Two other pieces of information should be considered: number of Hapax/Dis/Tris Legomena and their distribution in the corpus. This is something we have done in another publication (Delmonte, 1983), where we studied in detail Vocabulary Growth and distribution. I will include this study in another Table 3 below.

Table 2. Quantitative evaluation of Vocabulary Richness (1)

Poets/Occurrences	Tokens	Types	VR
Francis Webb	66965	12363	18.64
Anne Sexton	36501	5471	15.73
Emily Dickinson	31873	4503	14.13
T.S.Eliot	29144	5026	17.24
Sylvia Plath	28239	6166	21.84
Elizabeth Bishop	19047	4156	21.82
Robert Frost	21306	3251	15.26
Walt Whitman	76047	10946	14.39
W.B.Yeats	131485	10666	8.11
Wall Street Journal	1061166	28219	2.71
Total/Mean Poets	440607	62548	14.20

From Table 2., it is quite easy to see that Sylvia Plath has the highest ratio or VR, followed by Elizabeth Bishop, then Webb and Eliot. Other poets are placed lower in the graded scale and of course written prose is placed at the lowest. Even if VR computed with absolute number is not very indicative, we can easily see that Webb has the highest number of Types of all poets. In the following table we further deepen the study of Vocabulary Richness by examining Low Frequency Word distribution in the 6 poets. From Table 3. we can easily see that Plath corpus is now the poet with highest number of Hapax.

Table 3. Quantitative evaluation of Vocabulary Richness (2)

Poets/Occurrences	Hapax	Bis	Tris	Rare	Types	Hapax	Rare
Francis Webb	6662	1961	909	9532	12363	0.575	0.77
Anne Sexton	3144	924	395	4463	5471	0.575	0.81
Emily Dickinson	1716	1164	403	3283	4503	0.381	0.72
T.S.Eliot	2239	1365	366	3970	5026	0.445	0.79
Sylvia Plath	3686	982	384	5052	6166	0.598	0.82
Elizabeth Bishop	2471	631	334	3436	4156	0.594	0.82
Robert Frost	1730	548	240	2518	3251	0.532	0.77
Walt Whitman	5318	1753	845	7916	10946	0.486	0.72
W.B.Yeats	4698	1821	874	7393	10666	0.440	0.79
Total/Mean Poets	31664	11149	4750		62548	0.498	

This second Table evaluates Vocabulary Richness on the basis of words repeated only once, twice or three times, and Rare Words, that is their sum. From this second evaluation we see the primacy of Sylvia Plath and Elizabeth Bishop with the highest percentages of less repeated words. Values indicated in the column Hapax, when subtracted from 1, will give the socalled Repetition Rate, which is complementary to number of once words. However the computation still suffers from the influence of a Zipfian variable, that is, the fact that by increasing the number of occurrences or tokens, number of types are meant to decrease in an incremental fashion. To better understand this point we should have made available for all poets, the Table of Vocabulary Increase which is however only available for Webb and has appeared in one of my previous publications (Delmonte 1980). We report this table together with the values of Standard Deviations for the six Phases or Folds into which Webb's corpus had been subdivided. Consider that these data are slightly different from current ones, because they were derived from previous version of Collected Poems.

Table 4. Vocabulary Increase in Webb's Poetic Corpus

Types/Phase	Ph1	Ph2	Ph3	Ph4	Ph5	Ph6	Total
Tokens	10540	10540	10540	10540	10540	10538	63238
Types	3606	3526	3260	3096	3626	3205	20319
New Words	1422	1276	1189	999	1401	1144	7431
Hapax Leg.	1246	1151	1089	897	1263	1021	6667

Table 5. Vocabulary Increase in Webb's Poetic Corpus expressed in Standard Error

Types/Phase	Ph1	Ph2	Ph3	Ph4	Ph5	Ph6
Types	.884	.181	-.239	-1.154	.783	-.455
New Words	.915	.270	-.158	-1.454	1.031	-.612
Hapax Leg.	.287	.183	-.165	-.380	.314	-.238

As can be easily gathered from these Tables, 4. and 5., Vocabulary Increase has been quite high in the first two Phases of Webb's poetic production, and in the second last. It suffered a slow down in the other three Phases, but was nonetheless quite sustained.

As a final note, I consider Webb's poetic production always very innovative, imaginative and full of inspiration. The vocabulary he used was always very appropriate to the theme and style of the poem.

Here below is a semantic evaluation of his poetry: I also wanted to account for the use of semantically positive vs negative words in Webb's poetry, even if just with simple counts, and we show the results in the following section.

5.6 Metaphors, Positive vs Negative Images

Affective valency is a very common research area and theme in Information Retrieval and Computational Linguistic in general. In order to account for Webb's use of affective vocabulary, I collected a list of what I regard positive vs negative words used in Collected Poems. I also collected separately, words which I see as neutral in their affective valency. I present the lists and the occurrencies counts. The results are quite interesting and confirm the idea that Francis Webb was a positive, optimistic visionary.

POSITIVE WORDS – Total Counts = 1763

good, silver, gold, warm, white, star, dawn, sun, moon, light, morning, day, green, bright, clear, brilliant, love, joy, pure, birth, born, life, sleep, mother, father, friend, bless, truth, laughter, flower, holy, grace, passion, summer

NEGATIVE WORDS – Total Counts = 1469

bad, mist, cold, grey, fog, dark, cloud, black, twilight, sunset, sundown, shade, nightfall, night, hate, gloom, dusk, dim, grief, wreck, blood, bleed, die, death, dead, pain, false, pale, ghost, pity, shiver, winter

Words have been counted considering their possible inflections and derivations. And of course homographs have been eliminated from the count. It would seem that number of inherently positive words are higher than negative ones.

Francis Webb's poetry is full of metaphors, similes and other rhetorical devices that we will look into more deeply in this section. Extended or explicit metaphors are enacted in a poem basically by the use of two grammatical linguistic markers: LIKE and AS. These two conjunctions are the intermediary linguistic and grammatical means to assert the poet's presence, his/her command of the communicative goal the poem may have in the reader. In other words they make patent, apparent the presence of the point of view of the poet. In Table 5. we present data from a number of contemporary poets which have been partly made object of enquiry in previous works by myself [4,5]. An important contribution by Kaplan's APSA, was making available corpora of a number of American poets which we may now compare to Webb in order to better evaluate the linguistic properties of his work. In the same Table I also added figures for the use of the two other conjunctions, AND/OR which are commonly used to conjoin or disjoin alternate linguistic items in normal prose writing. This is not so in poetry and Webb uses the two conjunctions as a substitute to a null marker of adjacency: two or more concepts are thus juxtaposed to communicate synaesthetic images by means of asyndetons. There is no room here to show examples but it is quite normal that poets coordinate or disjoint images rather than concepts or semantic propositions in their poems.

The other important component that is used by Webb to produce metaphors are list structures, that is images or concepts separated by commas repeated in a sequence of two or three. We counted both single words and also two words or bigrams, again separated by commas in a sequence. This is an artifice that achieves the same result of asyndetic juxtaposition by proposing parallel structures to the reader.

Table 5.1 Grammatical Markers for Metaphor and Synaesthesia

Poets/Markers	LIKE	AS	AND	OR	LISTS
Francis Webb	221	345	2355	251	298
Anne Sexton	170	148	643	63	66
Emily Dickinson	49	135	390	78	61
T.S.Eliot	26	54	651	107	124
Sylvia Plath	111	93	404	44	118
Elizabeth Bishop	124	83	656	110	61

Robert Frost	86	167	72	78	49
Walt Whitman	37	245	1757	301	925
Total	824	1270	6928	1032	1702

In Table 5. we show absolute and weighted frequency values of the occurrence of the conjunctions used to objectively build metaphors. If we look at totals, we understand that Francis Webb is the poet that uses most of explicit markers, like/as. Together with Whitman, they are the two poets using most similar devices. However absolute counts need to be interpreted and relativized in order to acquire a comparable value, and this is done by weighting absolute figures by the number of types making up their corpus of poems.

Table 5.2 Grammatical Markers for Metaphor and Synaesthesia

Poets/Markers	Total Like/As	Ratio WMM	Total And/Or
Francis Webb	566	30.36	139.81
Anne Sexton	318	20.21	44.88
Emily Dickinson	184	13.02	33.12
T.S.Eliot	80	4.64	43.91
Sylvia Plath	204	9.34	20.51
Elizabeth Bishop	207	9.49	35.11
Robert Frost	253	16.58	9.83
Walt Whitman	282	19.60	143.02
Total	2094	2094	7950
Mean	261.7	261.7	993.7

Weighted Mean	15.60	15.60	59.23

This is what we do in the two final columns where we report the ratio of absolute totals by the value of Vocabulary Richness that is computed in the section below, dedicated to quantitative measurements. Weighted Metaphor Markers (or WMM for short) indicate clearly Webb's primacy in the richness of explicit metaphoric constructs as testified by the amount of LIKE and AS occurrences. In fact, the same applies to the other two conjunctions: Webb is by far the most frequent user followed by Whitman. List structure on the contrary are found in a greater number in Whitman followed by Webb. Another syntactic construction often used to produce metaphoric meaning is by copulative structure, where the conjuncts like/as are omitted, thus generating a "strange" property assignment process to the subject of the copula.

5.7 A Statistical Evaluation of Personal Pronoun Distribution

In our previous edition we produced a statistical evaluation of the distribution of two pronouns "I" and "We" in Webb's poetry. We did that by dividing the collected poems into 6 phases which were however unbalanced as to the number of words contained in each phase. The study was produced in 1978 using a Cray mainframe computer connected in batch mode to Venice at the Computing Center of Ca Foscari University, by a program written in Fortran on punched cards.

The computing situation has completely changed and it is very easy to reproduce the same experiment on any laptop by means of a simple text editor counting occurrences and then producing the table and diagram under any spreadsheet. Our new version of the analysis takes into account 4 different pronoun series and applies the study to the six phases computed this time by keeping each phase as close as possible to the same quantity of words. Since the collected poems contain some 67000 words each phase must have 11000 words approximately. And this is what we have done and the results are very interesting as they were in the previous study. So first of all the pronouns and adjectives we analyzed are the following ones:

FirstPersonSingular:
I, MY, MINE, ME

SecondPerson:
YOU, YOUR, YOURS

FirstPersonPlural:
WE, US, OUR, OURS

ThirdPersonPlural:
THEY, THEM, THEIR, THEIRS

As appears, we added possessives and clitic complement pronouns to subject pronouns we used previously and this has been done in order to capture all possible reference to the person of the poet or the persona. The use of "I" indicates a tendency to concentrate on the self: I called the value obtained by dividing up the number of FirstPersonSingular pronouns by the number of FirstPersonPlural "the coefficient of egocentricity". In the previous study this coefficient indicated a predominance of the singular in Phase 3 and in Phase 4 where the value was slightly lower. The current study reiterates the same situation, but it adds more information as to the role of the other personal pronouns.

As can be seen in the table and the diagram below, the use of the egocentric "I" remains fairly high also in the following phases, Phase 5 and 6. It is also interesting to note the peak of the second person pronoun in Phase 4. First person plural "WE" increase remarkably in Phase 6, that is the opposite of what happens to the egocentric pronoun "I" which decreases, showing an openness to embrace the others. In fact the two pronouns reach almost the same position on the diagram balancing their impact on the self of the poet. Another interesting data is represented by the increase of the ThirdPersonPlural which again shows an increase in the last phase corroborating the analysis proposed before.

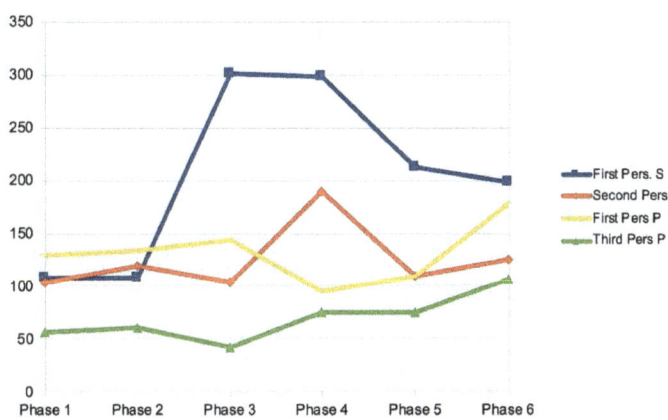

Figure 1. Distribution of Personal Pronouns into Six Phases

We report below the table containing the actual data in their absolute values. For each Phase and Type of data we also computed Mean and Standard Deviations. As can be noticed, the value of Standard Deviation is fairly high for FirstPersonSingular and is very low for the Plural pronouns, notwithstanding the identical value of their Mean.

This difference is the cause of the peaks in the two central phases

Table 6. Quantitative Analysis of Four Personal Pronouns

	First Pers. S	Second Pers	First Pers P	Third Pers P	Totals
Phase 1	108	104	130	56	398
Phase 2	108	120	133	61	422
Phase 3	301	104	144	42	591
Phase 4	299	189	95	75	658
Phase 5	213	110	110	75	508
Phase 6	198	125	178	106	607
Totals	1227	752	790	415	3184
Means	153	114,5	154	81	
Stand.Dev.	63,6396103	14,8492424	33,9411255	35,3553391	

CHAPTER VI: COMPUTATIONAL ANALYSIS OF WEBB'S CORPUS

6.1 SPARSAR - Automatic Analysis of Poetic Structure and Rhythm with Syntax, Semantics and Phonology

This chapter is made possible by the creation of a system for poetry analysis which took many years to realize called SPARSAR[33]. The system produces a deep analysis of each poem at different levels: it works at sentence level at first, than at verse level and finally at stanza level (see Figure 1 below). The structure of the system is organized as follows: at first syntactic, semantic and grammatical functions are evaluated. Then the poem is translated into a phonetic form preserving its visual structure and its subdivision into verses and stanzas. Phonetically translated words are associated to mean duration values taking into account position in the word and stress. At the end of the analysis of the poem, the system can measure the following parameters: mean verse length in terms of msec. and in number of feet. The latter is derived by a verse representation of metrical structure.

Another important component of the analysis of rhythm is constituted by the algorithm that measures and evaluates rhyme schemes at stanza level and then the overall rhyming structure at poem level. As regards syntax, we now have at our disposal, chunks and dependency structures if needed. To complete our work, we introduce semantics both in the version of a classifier and by isolating verbal complex in order to verify propositional properties, like presence of negation, computing factuality from a crosscheck with modality,

---

[33] See Delmonte R. (2013). SPARSAR: a System for Poetry Automatic Rhythm and Style AnalyzeR, SLATE 2013, Demonstration Track, and a long list of following papers showing progress in the ability of the system to represent poetic devices and content,

aspectuality – that we derive from our lexica – and tense. On the other hand, the classifier has two different tasks: distinguishing concrete from abstract nouns, identifying highly ambiguous from singleton concepts (from number of possible meanings from WordNet and other similar repositories). Eventually, we carry out a sentiment analysis of every poem, thus contributing a three-way classification: neutral, negative, positive that can be used as a powerful tool for evaluation purposes.

We have been inspired by by Kaplan's tool APSA[34], and started developing a system with similar tasks, but which was more transparent and more deeply linguistically-based. The main new target in our opinion, had to be an index strongly semantically based, i.e. a "Semantic Density Index" (SDI). With this definition I now refer to the idea of classifying poems according to their intrinsic semantic density in order to set apart those poems which are easy to understand from those that require a rereading and still remain somewhat obscure. An intuitive notion of SDI can be formulated as follow:

- easy to understand are those semantic structures which contain a proposition, made of a main predicate and its arguments
- difficult to understand are on the contrary semantic structures which are filled with nominal expressions, used to reinforce a concept and are juxtaposed in a sequence
- also difficult to understand are sequences of adjectives and nominals used as modifiers, union of such items with a dash.

There are other elements that I regard very important in the definition of semantic parameters and are constituted by presence of negation and modality: this is why we compute Polarity and Factuality. Additional features are obtained by measuring the level of affectivity by means of sentiment analysis, focussing on presence of negative

---

[34] See Kaplan, D. (2006). Computational analysis and visualized comparison of style in American poetry. Unpublished undergraduate thesis.

items which contribute to make understanding more difficult.

The Semantic Density Index is derived from the computation of a number of features, some of which have negative import while others positive import. At the end of the computation the index may end up to be positive if the poem is semantically "light", that is easy to read and understand; otherwise, it is computed as "heavy" which implies that it is semantically difficult.

At the end we come up with a number of evaluation indices that include: a Constituent Density Index, a Sentiment Analysis Marker, a Subjectivity and Factuality Marker. We also compute a Deep Conceptual Index, see below.

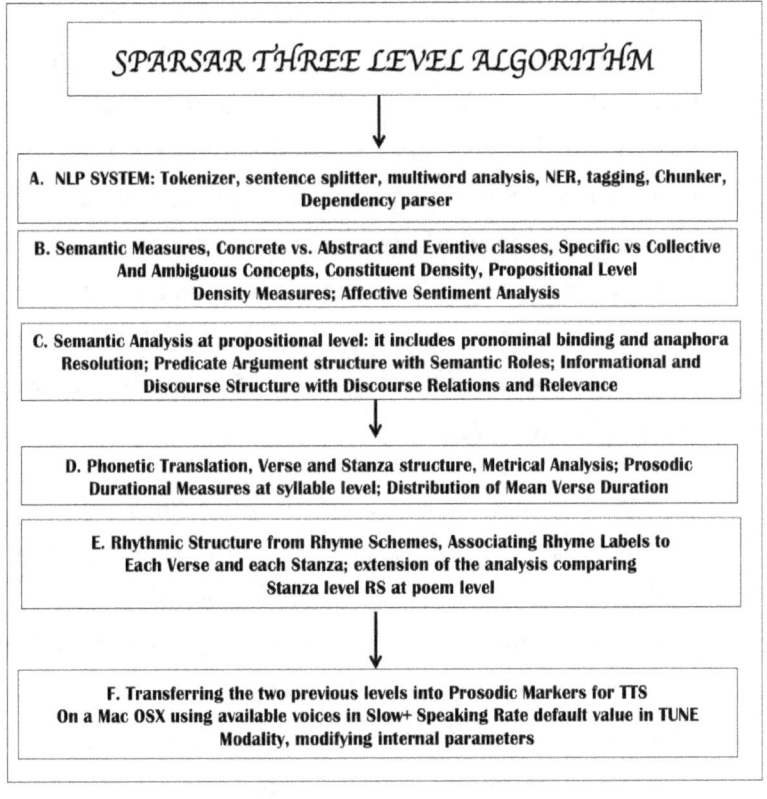

Figure 2. The SPARSAR three-level system

The procedure is based on the tokenized sentence, which is automatically extracted and may contain many verses up to a punctuation mark, usually period. Then I use the functional structures which are made of a head and a constituent which are measured for length in number of tokens. A first value of SDI comes from the proportion of verbal compounds and non-verbal ones. I assume that a "normal" distribution for a sentence corresponds to a semantic proposition that contains one verbal complex with a maximum of four non verbal structures. More verbal compounds contribute to reducing the SDI.

The other contribution comes from lemmatization and the association of a list of semantic categories, general semantic classes coming from WordNet or other similar computational lexica. These classes are also called supersense classes. As a criterion for grading difficulty, I consider more difficult to understand a word which is specialized for a specific semantic domain and has only one such supersense label. On the contrary, words or concepts easy to understand are those that are ambiguous between many senses and have more semantic labels associated to the lemma. A feature derived from quantitative linguistic studies is the rare words, which are those words that appear with less than 4 occurrences in frequency lists. I use the one derived from Google GigaWord.

The index will have a higher value for those cases of high density and a lower value for the contrary. It is a linear computation and includes the following features: the ratio of number of words vs number of verbs; the ratio of number of verbal compounds vs non-verbal ones; the internal composition of non-verbal chunks: every additional content word increases their weight (functional words are not counted); the number of semantic classes. Eventually a single index is associated to the poem which should be able to differentiate those poems which are easy from the cumbersome ones.

What I do is dividing each item by the total number of tagged words and of chunks. In detail, I divide verbs found by the total number of tokens (the more the best); I divide adjectives found by the total number of tokens (the more the worst); I divide verb structures by the total number of chunks (the more the best); I divide inflected vs uninflected verbal compounds (the more the best); I divide nominal chunks rich in components: those that have more than 3 members (the more the worst); I divide semantically rich (with less semantic categories) words by the total number of lemmas (the more the worst); I count rare words (the more the worst); I count generic or collective referred concepts (the more the best); I divide specific vs ambiguous semantic concepts (those classified with more than two senses) (the more the worst); I count doubt and modal verbs, and propositional level negation (the more the worst); I divide abstract and eventive words vs concrete concepts (the more the worst); I compute sentiment analysis with a count of negative polarity items (the more the worst).

Another important index we implemented is the Deep Conceptual index, which is obtained by considering the proportion of Abstract vs Concrete words contained in the poem. This index is then multiplied with the Propositional Semantic Density which is obtained at sentence level by computing how many non verbal, and among the verbal, how many non inflected verbal chunks there are in a sentence.

6.2 Related Work and State of the Art

Computational work on poetry addresses a number of subfields which are however strongly related. They include automated annotation, analysis, or translation of poetry, as well as poetry generation, that we comment here below. Other common subfields regard automatic grapheme-to-phoneme translation for out of vocabulary words as discussed in (see Reddy et al., Dmitriy et al.) use CMU pronunciation dictionary to derive stress and rhyming information, and incorporate constraints on meter and rhyme into a machine translation system. There has also been some work on computational approaches to characterizing rhymes (Byrd et al.) and global properties of the rhyme network (see Sonderegger et al.) in English. Eventually, graphical visualization of poetic features.

Green et al. use a finite state transducer to infer syllable-stress assignments in lines of poetry under metrical constraints. They contribute variations similar to the schemes below, by allowing an optional inversion of stress in the iambic foot. This variation is however only motivated by heuristics, noting that "poets often use the word 'mother' (S* S) at the beginnings and ends of lines, where it theoretically should not appear." So eventually, there is no control of the internal syntactic or semantic structure of the newly obtained sequence of feet: the optional change is only positionally motivated.

They employ statistical methods to analyze, generate, and translate rhythmic poetry. They first apply unsupervised learning to reveal word-stress patterns in a corpus of raw poetry. They then use these word-stress patterns, in addition to rhyme and discourse models, to generate English love poetry. Finally, they translate Italian poetry into English, choosing target realizations that conform to desired rhythmic patterns. They, however, concentrate on only one type of poetic meter, the iambic pentameter. What's more, they use the audio transcripts - made by just one person - to create a syllable-based word-stress gold standard corpus for testing, made of some 70 lines taken from Shakespeare's sonnets. Audio transcripts[35] without supporting acoustic analysis is not always the best manner to deal with stress assignment in syllable positions which might or might not conform to a strict sequence of iambs. There is no indication of what kind of criteria have been used, and it must be noted that the three acoustic cues may well not be congruent (see Tsur, 2012). So eventually results obtained are rather difficult to evaluate. As the authors note, spoken recordings may contain lexical stress reversals and archaic pronunciations[36].

Their conclusion is that "this useful information is not available in typical pronunciation dictionaries". Further on, (p. 531) they comment "the probability of stressing 'at' is 40% in general, but this increases to 91% when the next word is 'the'." We assume that demoting or promoting word stress requires information which is context and syntactically dependent. Proper use of one-syllable words remains tricky. In our opinion, machine learning would need much bigger training data than the ones used by the authors for their experiment.

There's an extended number of papers on poetry generation starting from work documented in a number of publications by P. Gervás (2001, 2010) who makes use of Case Based Reasoning to induce the best line structure. Other interesting attempts are by Toivanen et al. who use a corpus-based approach to generate poetry in Finnish. Their idea is to contribute knowledge needed in content and form by meas of two separate corpora, one providing semantic content, and another grammatical and poetic structure. Morphological analysis and synthesis is used together with text-mining methods. Basque poetry generation is the topic of Agirrezabal et al. paper which uses POS-tags to induce the

---

[35] One questions could be "Has the person transcribing stress pattern been using pitch as main acoustic correlate for stress position, or loudness (intensity or energy) or else durational patterns?". The choice of one or the other acoustic correlates might change significantly the final outcome.

[36] At p.528 they present a table where they list a number of words - partly function and partly content words - associated to probability values indicating their higher or lower propensity to receive word stress. They comment that "Function words and possessives tend to be unstressed, while content words tend to be stressed, though many words are used both ways".

linear ordering and WordNet to select best semantic choice in context.

Manurung et al., (2000a,2000b) have explored the problem of poetry generation under some constraints using machine learning techniques. With their work, the authors intended to fill the gap in the generation paradigm, and "to shed some light on what often seems to be the most enigmatic and mysterious forms of artistic expression". The conclusion they reach is that "despite our implementation being at a very early stage, the sample output succeeds in showing how the stochastic hillclimbing search model manages to produce text that satisfies these constraints." However, when we come to the evaluation of metre we discover that they base their approach on wrong premises.

The authors quote the first line of what could be a normal limerick but get the metrical structure totally wrong. In limericks, what we are dealing with are not dactyls - TAtata - but anapests, tataTA, that is a sequence of two unstressed plus a closing stressed syllable. This is a well-known characteristic feature of limericks and the typical rhythm is usually preceded and introduced by a iamb "there ONCE", and followed by two anapests, "was a MAN", "from maDRAS". Here in particular it is the syntactic-semantic phrase that determines the choice of foot, and not the scansion provided by the authors[37].

Reddy & Knight produce an unsupervised machine learning algorithm for finding rhyme schemes which is intended to be language-independent. It works on the intuition that "a collection of rhyming poetry inevitably contains repetition of rhyming pairs. ... This is partly due to sparsity of rhymes – many words that have no rhymes at all, and many others have only a handful, forcing poets to reuse rhyming pairs." The authors harness this repetition to build an unsupervised algorithm

---

[37] "For instance, the line 'There /once was a /man from Ma/dras', has a stress pattern of (w,s,w,w,s,w,w,s). This can be divided into feet as (w),(s,w,w),(s,w,w),(s). In other words, this line consists of a single upbeat (the weak syllable before the first strong syllable), followed by 2 dactyls (a classical poetry unit consisting of a strong syllable followed by two weak ones), and ended with a strong beat."(ibid.7)

to infer rhyme schemes, based on a model of stanza generation. We test the algorithm on rhyming poetry in English and French." The definition of rhyme the authors used is the strict one of perfect rhyme: two words rhyme if their final stressed vowels and all following phonemes are identical. So no half rhymes are considered. Rhyming lines are checked from CELEX phonological database.

There's s small number of rule-based systems available for download which need to be considered before presenting our system, and they are – listed from the oldest to the latest:

– the Scandroid by C.Hartman (2004/5), downloadable at http://oak.conncoll.edu/cohar/Programs.htm, and presented in Hartman et al.;
– the Stanford Literary Lab by Algee-Hewitt, M.,Heuser, R. Kraxenberger, M., Porter, J., Sensenbaugh, J., and Tackett, J. (2014), downloadable at https://github.com/quadrismegistus/lit lab-poetry, and presented in Heuser 2005, Algee-Hewitt et al. 2014;
– the University of Toronto Canadian Representative Poetry Online project carried out by M.R. Plamondon and documented in Plamondon 2006, downloadable at Library website http://rpo.libr ary.utoronto.ca/;
– a collaborative effort carried out by American and German universities called MYOPIA, presented in Manish et al. 2012, and available at two websites by the main author Helen Armstrong, https://lecture2go.uni-hamburg.de/konferenzen/-/k/13930, http://www.helenarmstrong.us/desig n/myopia/;
– ZeuScansion for the scansion of English poetry by M. Agirrezabal et al. presented in Agirrezabal et al. 2013, and available at https://github.com/manexagirrezabal/zeuscansion;
– RhymeDesign a tool designed for the analysis of metric and

rhythmic devices, by N.McCurdy et al., a tool previously called Poemage, documented at http://www.sci.utah.edu/~nmccurdy /Poemage/ and now presented as project at http://ninamccurdy .com/?page_id=398.

A number of more or less recent works have addressed the problem related to rhyme identification, by Manish Chaturvedi et al. and by Karteek Addanki and Dekai Wu, but also previously by Hussein Hirjee and Daniel Brown and by Susan Bartlett et al.. Eventually a selected list of authors have specifically addressed the problem of visualization of linguistic and literary data in recent and not so recent works, notably on poetry visualization (see Raman et al. 2013), literary analysis and concordancing (see Keim et al 2007; Oelke et al, 2008; Wattenberg et al. 2008.

6.3 Indices and Graphical Display

Eventually, together with the indices indicated above, I devised four complex indices and the final best grading index to evaluate a poem. Another important index is the one represented by the Lexical Selection index which is a combination of Vocabulary Richness and the Rare Words, where the first is the ratio obtained between Types and Tokens, the second is the ratio obtained between Rare Words and Types. That is, with the first index we know how many single wordforms and no repetition are included in the poem, and with the second we learn how many types are rare words, i.e. are words that have frequency equal or below 3 in the general index of billion words obtained from the web and other such sources.

In the figures obtained by Kaplan's Poetry Analyzer we increased the weight associated to all rhyming devices which include the following: Alliteration Frequency; Assonance Frequency; Consonance Frequency; Slant End Rhyme Frequency; Semi End Rhyme Frequency; Perfect End Rhyme Frequency; Identity End Rhyme Frequency; Sound Devices Frequency; Partial End Rhyme Frequency; Full End Rhyme Frequency; End Rhyme Frequency. Without this modification the distribution of the poems in the space would look totally different, and this can be seen by comparing the two pictures below in Fig. 3 and 4: in the first one rhyming devices are set to zero; on the contrary, in the second picture the same parameters are risen to half their value. As can be seen, none of the poem preserves the same position apart from "The Gunner": curiously enough, the poem has also the same position in our system evaluation. The question is that this poem is a strongly rhymed structure of the AABB with full end rhymes and there is no reason why by modifying weights this feature does not also modify its position in the window. On the contrary, if we look at the output of our system, which will be shown in a section below, the rhyming feature is particularly highlighted and contributes a much higher value of metrical measure parameter. 'The Gunner" in fact is assigned totally different positions according to parameters evaluated.

As can be easily gathered, collapsing all parameters in one single value that is used to position the poem in the vector space is not the best practice because it obscures the specificity of the poem in terms of semantic and conceptual import, rather than rhetoric or rhyming devices. In Figure 3 below I show at first the map for 130 poems, that is the majority of Webb's poetic production, where poems clustering in the centre share similarities, while poems on the outskirt of the cloud are to be regarded as deviants.

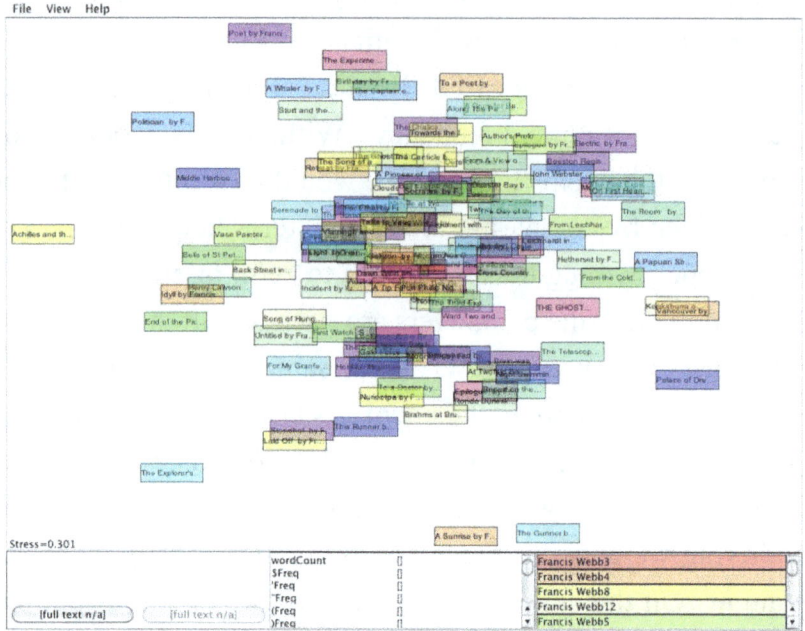

Figure 3. Map of 130 poems by Webb produced by APSA

Just to get an idea of what APSA system computes I include here below the list of parameters and their corresponding values for two poems, "Achilles and the Woman" and "Five Days Old".

Author|Title|wordCount|$Freq|'Freq|"Freq|(Freq|)Freq|,Freq|--Freq|?Freq|!Freq|.Freq|:Freq|;Freq|...Freq|CCFreq|CDFreq|DTFreq|EXFreq|FWFreq|INFreq|JJFreq|JJRFreq|JJSFreq|LSFreq|MDFreq|NNFreq|NNPFreq|NNPSFreq|properNounFreq|NNSFreq|PDTFreq|POSFreq|PRPFreq|PRP$Freq|RBFreq|RBRFreq|RBSFreq|RPFreq|SYMFreq|TOFreq|UHFreq|VBFreq|VBDFreq|VBGFreq|VBNFreq|VBPFreq|VBZFreq|WDTFreq|WPFreq|WP$Freq|WRBFreq|numLines|avgLineLength|1SGNFreq|2SGNFreq|3SGMFreq|3SGFFreq|3SGNFreq|1PLNFreq|2PLNFreq|3PLNFreq|contractionsFreq|avgWordLength|alliterationFreq|assonanceFreq|consonanceFreq|slantEndRhymeFreq|semiEndRhymeFr eq|perfectEndRhymeFreq|identityEndRhymeFreq|adjFreq|nounFreq|verbFreq|conjFreq|topNounFreq|topAdjFreq|topVerbFreq|numStanzas|avgLinesPerStanza|comparativesFreq|soundDevicesFreq|partialEndRhymeFreq|fullEndRhymeFreq|endRhymeFreq

Francis Webb|Achilles and the Woman
|0.40987654320987654|0.0|0.0|0.0|0.0|0.0|0.046875|0.0|0.0|0.0|0.0390625|0.0|0.0078125|0.0|0.0859375|0.0078125|0.109375|0.0078125|0.0|0.140625|0.078125|0.0078125|0.0|0.0|0.0|0.140625|0.0078125|0.0|0.0078125|0.0859375|0.0|0.0|0.078125|0.0390625|0.0234375|0.0|0.0|0.0|0.0|0.0234375|0.0|0.015625|0.0625|0.015625|0.0078125|0.0234375|0.0|0.0|0.0078125|0.0|0.015625|0.22222222222222224|0.4611111111111111|0.0859375|0.0234375|0.0|0.0|0.0|0.0|0.0|0.0078125|0.0|0.13177083333333334|0.023622047244094488|0.23622047244094488|0.4094488188976378|0.16666666666666666|0.0|0.1|0.0|0.09375|0.234375|0.1015625|0.2265625|0.015625|0.0078125|0.015625|0.15000000000000002|0.55|0.0078125|0.6692913385826771|0.16666666666666666|0.1|0.2666666666666666

Francis Webb |Five Days Old|0.4888888888888889|0.0|0.0|0.0|0.005208333333333333|0.005208333333333333|0.09375|0.0|0.015625|0.0|0.057291666666666664|0.005208333333333333|0.0|0.0|0.036458333333333336|0.0|0.088541666666666667|0.0|0.0|0.16666666666666666|0.08333333333333333|0.0|0.0|0.0|0.015625|0.19270833333333334|0.057291666666666664|0.0|0.057291666666666664|0.06770833333333333|0.005208333333333333|0.0|0.03125|0.036458333333333336|0.052083333333333336|0.0|0.0|0.0|0.0|0.020833333333333332|0.0|0.026041666666666668|0.020833333333333332|0.020833333333333332|0.026041666666666668|0.026041666666666668|0.020833333333333332|0.0|0.005208333333333333|0.0|0.0|0.475|0.25472972972972974|0.046875|0.010416666666666666|0.0|0.0|0.0|0.010416666666666666|0.0|0.0|0.0|0.225|0.031413612

565445025|0.38219895287958117|0.5602094240837696|0.09523809
523809523|0.0|0.08571428571428572|0.0|0.08333333333333333|0.31
77083333333333|0.09375|0.203125|0.005208333333333333|0.005208
333333333333|0.020833333333333332|0.4666666666666667|0.6083
333333333333|0.0|0.9738219895287958|0.09523809523809523|0.085
71428571428572|0.18095238095238095

In Figures 4 and 5 below I show the output of APSA system for those poems regarded as deviant in a previous graph, and produce an analysis where the poem positioned in centre space represent the norm and this is *Five Days Old*. The other poems are: *A Sunrise, The Gunner, The Explorer's Wife, For My Grandfather, Idyll, Middle Harbour, Politician, To a Poet, The Captain of the Oberon, Palace of Dreams, The Room, Vancouver by Rail, Henry Lawson, Achilles and the Woman.*

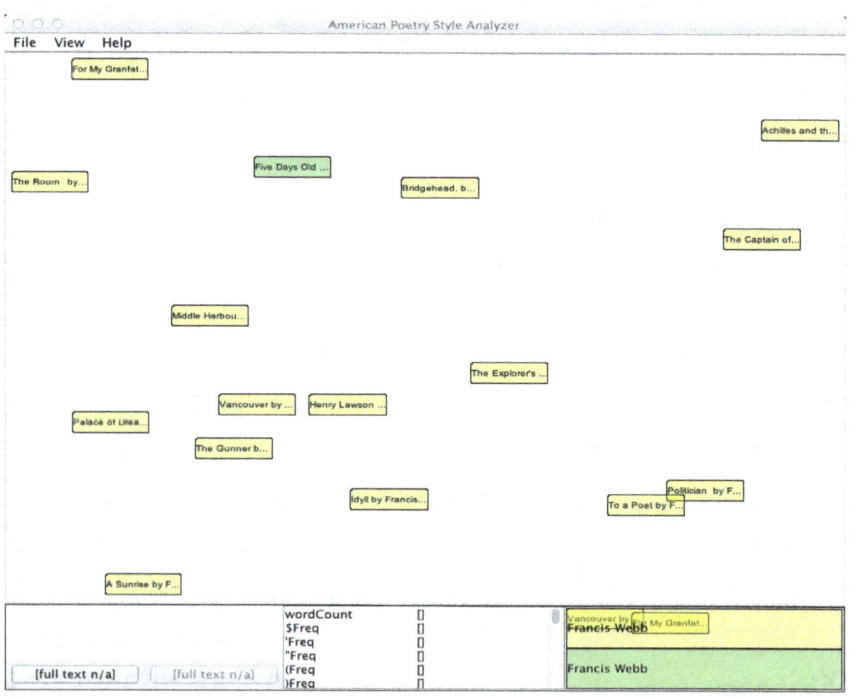

Figure 4. Francis Webb 15 deviant poems not filtered

In the APSA graphical spatial representation, the positioning of all poems starting from top of the window is almost totally different when modifying weights associated to Rhymes and other Rhetorical Devices. They can be listed as follows, where we collected labels associated to each coloured rectangle in the vertical order in which they appear. We then list in the third column the graded scale produced by our system. As can be easily gathered from Table 6, only four poems are graded the same by the two systems.

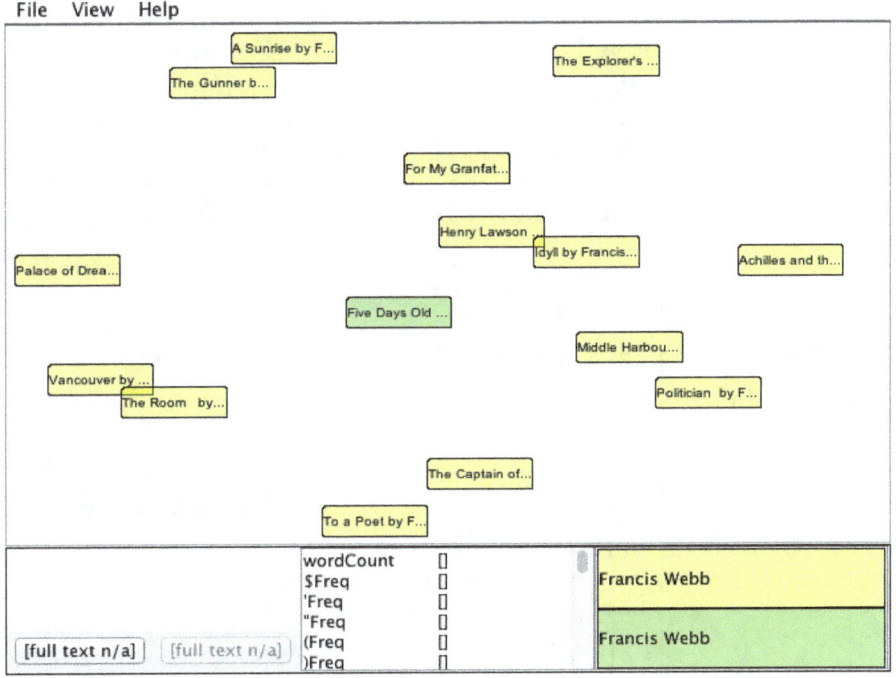

Figure 5. Francis Webb 15 deviant poems filtered by weights

If we look at Table 7 below, we discover then that poems are graded quite differently by SPARSAR depending on the indices involved.

Table 6. Comparing graded positions in space in APSA and in SPARSAR

Poems Graded the same in at least two scales	A. Figure 4. before weights	B. Figure 5. after weights	C. SPARSAR's grading
	For My Grandfather	Achilles	Middle Harbour
	Achilles	Politician	Bridgehead
	Five Days Old	Idyll	For My Grandfather
	The Room	The Captain	To a Poet
	Bridgehead	The Explorer's Wife	The Room
The Captain A/C	The Captain	Middle Harbour	The Captain
Henry Lawson B/C	Middle Harbour	Henry Lawson	Henry Lawson
	The Explorer's Wife	To a Poet	Idyll
Vancouver A/C	Vancouver by Rail	Bridgehead	Vancouver by Rail
	Henry Lawson	Five Days Old	A Sunrise

		Palace of Dreams	For My Grandfather	The Explorer's Wife
The Gunner A/B/C	The Gunner	The Gunner	The Gunner	
		Politician	A Sunrise	Achilles
		Idyll	Vancouver by Rail	Five Days Old
		To a Poet	The Room	Palace of Dreams
		A Sunrise	Palace of Dreams	Politician

Table 7. Comparing graded positions generated from indices computed by SPARSAR: headers stand for PRD=Poetic Rhetoric Devices, ML=Metrical Length, SD=Semantic Density, PSD=Prosodic Structure Distribution, DCI=Deep Conceptual Index

POEMS	PRD	ML	SD	PSD	DCI	Ident
Middle Harbour	2	5	9	7	7	X 7
Bridgehead	10	9	5	6	2	
Grandfather	7	8	10	13	12	
To a Poet	5	13	8	4	1	
The Room	4	15	1	3	3	X 3
The Captain	13	11	6	5	4	
Henry Lawson	1	16	7	1	6	X 1

Idyll	6	4	12	12	13	X 12
Vancouver	9	2	11	14	8	
A Sunrise	12	7	13	15	15	X 15
Explorer's Wife	8	6	2	16	9	
The Gunner	3	1	16	11	5	
Achilles	11	3	14	9	14	X 14
Five Days Old	15	14	3	10	10	X 10
Palace of Dreams	14	10	4	8	16	
Politician	16	12	15	2	11	

6.3 Rhetoric Devices, Metrical and Prosodic Structure

The second module takes care of rhetorical devices, metrical structure and prosodic structure. This time the file is read on a verse by verse level by simply collecting strings in a sequence and splitting verses at each newline character. In a subsequent loop, whenever two newlines characters are met, a stanza is computed. In order to compute rhetorical and prosodic structure we need to transform each word into its phonetic counterpart, by accessing the transcriptions available in the CMU dictionary. The Carnegie Mellon Pronouncing Dictionary is freely available online and includes American English pronunciation[38]. Kaplan reports the existence of another dictionary which is however no longer available.[39] The version of the CMU dictionary they are referring

---

[38] It is available online at <http://www.speech.cs.cmu.edu/cgi-bin/cmudict/>.
[39] Previously, data for POS were merged in from a different dictionary (MRC Psycholinguistic Database,

to is 0.4 and is the version based on phone/phoneme transcription.

Kaplan & Blei[40] in their longer paper specifies that "No extra processing is done to determine pronunciation ... so some ambiguities are resolved incorrectly." [ibid.p.42]. In fact what they are using is the phoneme version of the dictionary and not the syllabified one, which has also been increased by new words. We had available a syllable parser which was used to build the VESD database of English syllables [41]. So we started out with a much bigger pronunciation dictionary which covers 170,000 entries approximately.

Remaining problems to be solved are related to ambiguous homographs like "import" (verb) and "import" (noun) and are treated on the basis of their lexical category derived from previous tagging and Out Of Vocabulary Words (OOVW). As happens in Kaplan's system, if a word is not found in the dictionary, we also try different capitalizations, as well as breaking apart hyphenated words, and then we check at first for 'd, 's, and s' endings and try combining those sounds with the root word. The simplest case is constituted by differences in spelling determined by British vs. American pronunciation. This is taken care of by a dictionary of graphemic correspondences. However, whenever the word is not found we proceed by morphological decomposition, splitting at first the word from its prefix and if that still does not work, its derivational suffix. As a last resource, we use an orthographically based version of the same dictionary to try and match the longest possible string in coincidence with our OOVW. Then we deal with the remaining portion of word again by guessing its morphological nature, and if that fails we simply use our grapheme-to-phoneme parser. Here below are some of the

---

<http://lcb.unc.edu/software/multimrc/multimrc.zip>, which uses British English pronunciation)

[40] Kaplan, D., & Blei, D. (2007). A computational approach to style in American poetry. In *IEEE Conference on Data Mining*.

[41] Bacalu C., Delmonte R. (1999). Prosodic Modeling for Syllable Structures from the VESD - Venice English Syllable Database, in Atti 9° Convegno GFS-AIA, Venezia.

OOVWs we had to reconstruct by means of our recovery strategy which is indicated by showing the input word rejected by the dictionary lookup, then the word found by subtraction and the final output obtained by recomposition:

% wayfarer à [wayfare-[w_ey1f_eh1_r_r]],
% gangrened à [gangrene-[g_ae1_nr_ah0_n_d]],
% krog à [krog-g_r_aa1_g]
% copperplate à [copper-k_aa1_p_er_p_l_ey1_t],
% splendor à [splendour-[s_p_l_eh1_n_d_er]],
% filmy à [film-f_ih1_l_miy],
% seraphic à seraphine--> [s_e_r_a_ph_iy1_k]
% unstarred à [starred-[ah_n_s_t_aa1_r_d]]

Other words we had to reconstruct are: shrive, slipstream, fossicking, unplotted, corpuscle, thither, wraiths, etc. In some cases, the problem that made the system fail was the syllable which was not available in our database of syllable durations, VESD. This problem has been coped with by manually inserting the missing syllable and by computing its duration from the component phonemes, or from the closest similar syllable available in the database. We only had to add 12 new syllables for a set of approximately 1000 poems that the system computed.

6.4 Computing Metrical Structure and Rhyming Scheme

Any poem can be characterized by its rhythm which is also revealing of the poet's peculiar style. In turn, the poem's rhythm is based mainly on two elements: meter, that is distribution of stressed and unstressed syllables in the verse, presence of rhyming and other poetic devices like alliteration, assonance, consonance, enjambments, etc.

which contribute to poetic form at stanza level.

Traditionally, poetic meter is visualized by a sequence of signs, typically a straight line is used to indicate vowels of stressed syllables and a half circle is positioned on vowels of unstressed ones. The sequence of these sings makes up the foot and depending on number of feet one can speak of iambic, trochaic, anapestic, dactylic, etc. poetic style.

English poetry has been for centuries characterized by iambic pentameter, that is a sequence of five feet made of a couple of unstressed + stressed syllables. Modern English poetry on the contrary – after G.M.Hopkins – has adopted a variety of stanza schemes.

A poetic foot can be marked by a numerical sequence as for instance in Hayward[42] who uses "0" for unstressed and "1" for stressed syllables to feed a connectionist model of poetic meter from a manually transcribed corpus. There he also tries to state the view that poets are characterized by their typical meter and rhythm, which work as their fingerprint.

We also agree with this view, however, we would like to be more specific on the notion of rhythm that we intend to purport. We do that in two ways: by considering stanzas as structural units in which rhyming – if existent - plays an essential role. Secondly and foremost, in our view, a prosodic acoustic view needs to be implemented as well, if any precise definition of rhythm and style is the goal. Syllables are not just any combination of sounds, and their internal structure is fundamental to the nature of the poetic rhythm that will ensue. This is partly amenable to the use and exploitation of poetic devices, which we also intend to highlight in our system. But what is paramount in our

---

[42] Hayward, M. (1991). A connectionist model of poetic meter. Poetics, 20, 303-317.; Hayward, M. (1996). Application of a connectionist model of poetic meter to problems in generative metrics. Research in Humanities Computing 4. (pp. 185-192). Oxford: Clarendon Press.

description of rhythm, is the use of the acoustic parameter of duration. The use of duration will allow our system to produce a model of a poetry reader that we intend to implement in the future by speech synthesis. In our demo we will show how poems can be characterized by the use of rhythmic and stylistic features in a highly revelatory manner, by comparing metrically similar poems of the same poet and of different poets.

To this aim we assume that syllable acoustic identity changes as a function of three parameters:

- internal structure in terms of onset and rhyme which is characterized by number consonants, consonant clusters, vowel or diphthong
- position in the word, whether beginning, end or middle
- primary stress, secondary stress or unstressed

These data have been collected in a database called VESD (Venice English Syllable Database) to be used in the Prosodic Module of SLIM, a system for prosodic self-learning activities. Syllables have been collected from WSJCAM, the Cambridge version of the continuous speech recognition corpus produced from the Wall Street Journal, distributed by the Linguistic Data Consortium (LDC). We worked on a subset of 4165 sentences, with 70,694 words which constitute half of the total number of words in the corpus amounting to 133,080. We ended up with 113,282 syllables and 287,734 phones. The final typology is made up of 44 phones, 4393 syllable types and 11,712 word types. From word-level and phoneme-level transcriptions we produced syllables automatically by means of a syllable parser. The result was then checked manually.

The analysis in SPARSAR starts by translating every poem into its phonetic form: as said above, we used the CMU Pronouncing

Dictionary for North American English to translate words into phoneme sequences, augmented with words derived from work above[43]. In a second pass we try to build syllables starting from longest possible phone sequences to shortest one. This is done heuristically trying to match pseudo syllables with our syllable list. Matching may fail and will then result in a new syllable which has not been previously met. We assume that any syllable inventory will be deficient, and will never be sufficient to cover the whole spectrum of syllables available in the English language.

For this reason, we introduced a number of phonological rules to account for any new syllable that may appear. Duration values are derived by comparison with phonologically closest ones – for this we use place, manner of articulation as parameters. We assign mean duration values in msecs to all syllables considering position and stress. We also take advantage of syntactic information computed separately to highlight chunks' heads as produced by our bottomup parser. In that case, stressed syllables takes maximum duration value.

After reading out the whole poem on a verse by verse basis and having produces all phonemic transcription, we look for rhetoric devices. Here assonances, consonances, allitterations and rhymes are analysed and then evaluated. We introduce an important prosodic element: we produce a prosodic model of the poem and compute duration at verse level. This is done by associating durations at syllable level. In turn, these data are found by associating phonemes into syllables with our parser, which works on the basis of the phonological criterion of syllable wellformedness. Syllable structure requires a nucleus to be in place, then a rhyme with an onset and offset.

Durations have been recorded by means of a statistical study, with

---

[43] See also Delmonte, R., (2010), Prosodic tools for language learning, International Journal of Speech Technology. Volume 12 Number 4, pp.161 – 184.

three different word positions: beginning, middle and end position. They have also been collected according to a prosodic criterion: stressed and unstressed syllables. Each syllable has been recorded with three durational values in msec.: minimum, mean and maximum duration length, with a standard deviation. To produce our prosodic model we take mean durational values. We also select, whenever possible, positional and stress values. Of course, if a syllable duration value is not available for those parameters we choose the default value, that is unstressed. Then we compute metrical structure, that is the alternation of beats: this is computed by considering all function or grammatical words which are monosyllabic as unstressed. We associate a "0" to all unstressed syllables, and a value of "1" to all stressed syllables, thus including both primary and secondary stressed syllables.

Durations are then collected at stanza level and a statistics is produced. Metrical structure is used to evaluate statistical measures for its distribution in the poem. As can be easily gathered from our transcription, it is difficult to find verses with identical number of syllables, identical number of metrical feet and identical metrical verse structure. If we consider the sequence "01" as representing the typical iambic foot, and the iambic pentameter as the typical verse metre of English poetry, in our transcription it is easy to see that there is no line strictly respecting it. On the contrary we find trochees, "10", dactyls, "100", anapests, "001"and spondees, "11". At the end of the computation, the system is able to measure two important indices: "mean verse length" and "mean verse length in no. of feet" that is mean metrical structure.

Additional measure that we are now able to produce are related to rhyming devices. Since we intended to take into account structural internal rhyming scheme and their persistence in the poem we enriched our algorithm with additional data. These measures are then accompanied by information derived from two additional component: word repetition and rhyme repetition at stanza level. Sometimes also refrain may apply, that is the repetition of an entire line of verse. Rhyming schemes together with metrical length, are the strongest parameters to consider when assessing similarity between two poems.

Eventually also stanza repetition at poem level may apply: in other words, we need to reconstruct the internal structure of metrical devices used by the poet. We then use this information as a multiplier. The final score is then tripled in case of structural persistence of more than one rhyming scheme; for only one repeated rhyme scheme, it is doubled. With no rhyming scheme there will be no increase in the linear count of rhetorical and rhyming devices.

Creating the rhyming scheme is not an easy task. We do that by a sequence of incremental steps that assign labels to each couple of rhyming line and then matches their output. To create rhyme schemes we need all last phonetic words coming from our previous analysis. We then match recursively each final phonetic word with the following ones, starting from the closest to the one that is 6 lines far apart. Each time we register the rhyming words and their distance, accompanied by an index associated to verse number. Stanza boundaries are not registered in this pass.

The following pass must reconstruct the actual final verse numbers and then produce an indexed list of couples, Verse Number-Rhyming Verse for all the verses, stanza boundaries included. Eventually, we associate alphabetic labels to the each rhyming verse starting from A to Z. A simple alphabetic incremental mechanism updates the rhyme label. This may go beyond the limits of the alphabet itself and in that case, double letter are used.

I distinguish between poems divided up into stanzas and those that have no such a structure. Then I get stanzas and their internal structure in term of rhyming labels. Eventually what I want to know is the persistence of a given rhyme scheme, how many stanza contain the same rhyme scheme and the length of the scheme. A poem with no rhyme scheme is much poorer than a poem that has at least one, so this needs to be evaluated positively and this is what I do. In the final evaluation, it is possible to match different poems on the basis of their rhetorical and rhyming devices, besides their semantic and conceptual indices.

Parameters related to the Rhyming Scheme (RS) contribute a multiplier to the already measured metrical structure which as we already noted is extracted from the following counts: a count of metrical feet and its distribution in the poem; a count of rhyming devices and their distribution in the poem; a count of prosodic evaluation based on durational values and their distribution. Now the RS is yet another plane or dimension on the basis of which a poem is evaluated. It is based on the regularity in the repetition of a rhyming scheme across the stanzas or simply the sequence of verses in case the poem is not divided up into stanzas. We don't assess different RSs even though we could: the only additional value is given by the presence of a Chain Rhyme scheme, that is a rhyme present in one stanza which is inherited by the following stanza. Values to be computed are related to the Repetition Rate (RR), that is how many rhymes are repeated in the scheme or in the stanza: this is a ratio between number of verses and their rhyming types. For instance, a scheme like AABBCC, has a higher repetition rate (corresponding to 2) than say AABCDD (1.5), or ABCCDD (1.5). So the RR is one parameter and is linked to the length of the scheme, but also to the number of repeated schemes in the poem: RS may change during the poem and there may be more than one scheme.

Different evaluation are given to full rhymes, which add up the number of identical phones, with respect to half-rhymes which on the contrary count only half that number. The final value is obtained by dividing up the RR by the total number of lines and multiplying by 100, and then summing the same number of total lines to the result. This is done to balance the difference between longer vs. shorter poems, where longer poems are rewarded for the intrinsic difficulty of maintaining identical rhyming schemes with different stanzas and different vocabulary.

We show now a number of examples from Francis Webb's poetry taken from Collected Poems cited above.

First example is "Morgan's Country" which is written in Dante's "terza rima" in tercets, the rhyming pattern is "a-b-a, b-c-b, c-d-c, etc." using chain rhymes. The poem is made up of 8 stanzas with the previous scheme and two ending stanzas which break it: the nineth stanzas introduces rhymes which are not present in the other stanzas, while the tenth stanza is made of two verses or a couplet, where the second verse repeats words contained in the first stanza of the poem, which we show here below:

First stanza:

> This is Morgan's country: now steady, Bill.
> (Stunted and grey, hunted and murderous.)
> Squeeze for the first pressure. Shoot to kill.
> …..

Two last stanzas:

> Seven: and a blaze fiercer than the sun.
> The wind struggles in the arms of the starved tree,
> The temple breaks on a threadbare mat of grass.

Eight: even under the sun's trajectory
This country looks grey, hunted and murderous.

Another interesting poem is "Before Two Girls" which is made up of six stanzas each of nine verses. The internal structure of the stanzas are characterized by iambic pentameters and sometimes alexandrines, apart from the sixth line which is always trimeter, that is three feet or six syllables. Here below I show the second and third stanzas:

For Jack and Jill, tumbling in the kennel or the stews
Take dust to bed with them under a consumptive moon
Choking in the heavens, or under a smoggy sun
And frayed counterpane of cloud. But the moon for man
Still goads the spavined panther, the ocean, claws
By proxy every coast
To reclaim for a flowering all that she can of dust.
And dust we become. Was it a whisper or a nothing
Came from our dust before His touch or His breathing?

Moist spot on the lung burning at compline, and burning
In the thorax of dawn: all deathbeds are gathering in
Around these two, and the rheum and haze of sin.
Darkness the sun, the moon. Time has begun.
For He is His pattern: one prayer, twisting and turning
Among the amphibious pleading
Forms and faces, compels the waters and the bleeding
Of His Heart: as for ever the mangled hands and breast
May ponder into flower the hot tumuli of dust.

Rhymes are not always isomorphic nor isometric as can be seen in the previous two stanzas. There are perfect or full rhymes for instance in the lines ending in "burning"/"turning" and also "in"/"sin". But then there are half-rhymes in the lines ending in "coast"/"dust", "sun"/"man", "stews"/"claws". Rhyme patterns vary in the first five lines, but are consistent in the last four. The poem repeats always the scheme ABCCADDEE; but the second stanza has another pattern in the first five lines: ABCDAEEFF and we report it below. It must be noted however that the poem contains a lot of repetition, which are centered around the word "dust", which is repeated 12 times and in one case it is made to rhyme with "lust". And the second stanza repeats "to be", to half-rhyme with the previous ending in "knowingly":

If they have finished the dishes and are leaning
Together in some timidity for the eye
Of the box–camera to wink at them, knowingly
Some chinaware chuckles, *It had to be, to be.*
They forsook the amorous dust for immaculate Meaning,
Only to find that same dust
Swarming fog–silken, making faces in its lust
(But faces melting into pity, irresolution, loss)
 All about the pure intimacy of the Faucet, the Cross.

So, in this case, the computation of rhyming schemes will end up with two different values. But there also poems with no rhyme scheme at all, or only limited to some of the lines in a stanza as for instance in "Ball's Head Again". In this poem there are four stanzas each one made up of a different number of lines: 13, 15, 22 and 23 lines. Each stanza uses different internal rhyming schemes which are however not repeated in the following stanza. So the final count the system makes is that there are 4 different rhyming schemes which have internal rhymes. Also the internal metrical structure is highly diversified or heterometric: it goes from pentameters to monometer.

"Nuriootpa" is a limerick dedicated to the wine valley: its rhyming scheme is AABBA as required, and also the contents are structures as the limerick requires. First line presents a character the second adds something he/she did, then two following lines insert some comments and elaborations, and there's a final line which ends the story. Here is one stanza:

> Men with ancient communal brooms last night
> Went over their pride and joy to doll it up aright.
> Interloping box and bottle,
> Some stray native head of cattle,
>   Were worried away or chivvied out of sight.

    All lines have an internal metrical structure based on the iambic pentameter but with 11 or sometimes 12 syllables, apart from the fifth line which is trimeter with seven syllables. Special structure is represented by "Foreword" and "Yellowhammer". The first poem is organized in three stanzas each 14 lines long. The internal rhyming scheme is represented by a complex but highly repetitive alternate structure, ABABCDBBCDEFEF, where full rhymes are sometimes accompanied by half-rhymes. Here is one stanza:

> We do not forget how to kill.
> Our classroom is clean, quite old,
> So demurely practical
> And exquisitely patrolled
> By so many teachers—by one
> Teacher. His accent, occasion
> May vary; not themes of his world.
> Tamed, compromising, cold,
> The Outside with its lightning and sun
> Surrenders all playtime passion
> To sidle through well–scrubbed glass.
> Few foreign trifles are hidden
> Under our desks, and to pass

Notes is strictly forbidden.

All lines have a trimeter feet structure with 7/8 syllables. "The Yellowhammer" also has three 13 lines stanzas and a final 11 lines stanza, with complex rhyming schemes: ABCDDCEFGFGFE, ABCDDBEEFGHHG, ABCDCEFGCGHHF, ABACDCDEBBE. Another interesting case is represented by "The Runner" which is organized in two octaves, but rhymes do not follow the "ottava rima" scheme. They are organized in couplets in full and half-rhymes. Here is one stanza:

Watch, and for a moment pace him on.
Clipped are the wings of space from him, and gone
Thrust from the hips, self–conscious overstride.
His face hangs yellow, curtainless and void
As a cracked window in a headlong shack.
Brushed by the terrible hammer of the track,
The little spider of torment kicks and swings
    In the grey, collapsing bubble of his lungs.

Finally we report another case of octave stanza poem, "Around Costessey – The Horses", where the rhyme scheme is again different from the expected alternate one, and is: AABCCBDD, where there are four rhyme types rather than only three as the traditional "ottava rima". The metrical structure is iambic pentameter as usual, with more than ten syllable however; and there are two lines which are trimeter, with 7 syllables, the fourth and the last line. Here is one stanza:

The vegetative soul is the dedicated rhetorician:
Yellow knuckles of gorse are eloquent; motion
Is the psyche entire whose fullness is a naked growing
Ungirt with passion or reflection.
Grass meanders intoxicate in green simple action,

Little hills troll the pastoral catches, allowing
Hosannas of Saints in sober gesture alive
As flowering cherry along a drive.

6.5 Computing Phonetic and Prosodic Structure

Here below some excerpts from a short poem "The Runner" where each word is followed by its phone representation after a slash:

0 the/dh_ah runner/r_ah1_n_er
1
2 watch/w_aa1_ch and/ah_n_d for/f_ao_r a/ah moment/m_ow1_m_ah_n_t pace/p_ey1_s him/hh_ih1_m on/aa_n
3 clipped/k_l_ih1_p_t are/aa_r the/dh_ah wings/w_ih1_ng_z of/ah_v space/s_p_ey1_s from/f_r_ah1_m him/hh_ih1_m and/ah_n_d gone/g_ao1_n
4 thrust/th_r_ah1_s_t from/f_r_ah1_m the/dh_ah hips/hh_ih1_p_s self/s_eh1_l_f conscious/k_aa1_n_sh_ah_s overstride/ow_v_s_t_r_ay1_d
5 his/hh_ih1_z face/f_ey1_s hangs/hh_ae1_ng_z yellow/y_eh1_l_ow curtainless/k_er1_t_ah_n_l_eh1_s and/ah_n_d void/v_oy1_d
6 as/ae_z a/ah cracked/k_r_ae1_k_t window/w_ih1_n_d_ow in/ih1_n a/ah headlong/hh_eh1_d_l_ao2_ng shack/sh_ae1_k
7 brushed/b_r_ah1_sh_t by/b_ay the/dh_ah terrible/t_eh1_r_ah_b_ah_l hammer/hh_ae1_m_er of/ah_v the/dh_ah track/t_r_ae1_k
8 the/dh_ah little/l_ih1_t_ah_l spider/s_p_ay1_d_er of/ah_v torment/t_ao1_r_m_eh2_n_t kicks/k_ih1_k_s and/ah_n_d swings/s_w_ih1_ng_z

stanza no. 1 verse durations
[1998.27, 2534.2, 2871.87, 2651.1,1951.35,2004.04,2653,2140.34]
total syllable length 18804.170000000002
mean verse length 2350.5212500000002
standard deviation 365.4796116821
skewness 0.13034352150269
kurtosis -1.8094344468253

verse no. 1. number of feet 4 total syllable length 12 metrical structure
[1,0,0,0,0,0,1,0,0,1,1,0]
verse no. 2. number of feet 6 total syllable length 18 metrical structure
[1,0,0,0,0,1,0,0,0,1,0,1,0,1,0,0,1,0]
verse no. 3. number of feet 6 total syllable length 17 metrical structure
[1,0,1,0,0,0,1,0,0,1,1,0,0,0,0,1,0]
verse no. 4. number of feet 7 total syllable length 13 metrical structure
[1,1,1,0,1,0,1,0,0,1,0,0,1]
verse no. 5. number of feet 6 total syllable length 13 metrical structure
[0,0,1,1,0,1,0,1,0,1,0,1,0]
verse no. 6. number of feet 4 total syllable length 14 metrical structure
[1,0,0,0,1,0,0,1,0,0,0,0,0,1]
verse no. 7. number of feet 6 total syllable length 20 metrical structure
[0,0,1,0,0,1,0,0,0,1,0,0,1,0,1,0,0,1,0,0]
verse no. 8. number of feet 7 total syllable length 14 metrical structure
[1,0,0,1,0,1,0,0,1,1,0,0,1,1]

stanza feet pattern [4,6,6,7,6,4,6,7]

stanza no. 2 verse durations
[2061.04, 2085.16, 2775.689, 1847.87, 1992.52, 2689.51, 2061.01, 2089.08]
total syllable length 17601.88
mean verse length 2200.235
standard deviation 338.5265626632
skewness 0.908373079126
kurtosis -0.98413459072

Eventually we produce the overall stanza feet pattern that we then use to compute the overall metrical structure.

stanza feet pattern [5,5,5,5,7,5,5,5]
mean verse length 2275.3781249999997
standard deviation 349.05328046433

skewness 0.503463090507
kurtosis -1.506168632999
mean verse length in no. of feet 5.5
standard deviation 0.9660917830792
skewness 0.22180678693147
kurtosis -1.010204081632

Additional measure that we are now able to produce are related to rhyming devices and they are for this poem:

Absolute Count of Rhyming Devices = 129.5
Ratio of Absolute Count by No of Stanzas = 0.017857142857142856
Ratio of RhDevs Absolute Count by Corrected No of Verses = 8.09375
Ratio of RhDevs Absolute Count by Repetition Rate = 198.14207650273224
Ratio of RhDevs Absolute Count by Rare Word Repetition Rate = 136.53804347826087
Ratio of RhDevs Absolute Count by No Tokens = 56.93040864574422

And then the Rhyming Schemes:

Stanza-based Rhyme Schemes
[1-[1-a,2-b,3-c,4-c,5-d,6-d,7-e,8-e],2-[10-f,11-f,12-g,13-g,14-h,15-h,16-i,17-i]]
Different Rhyme Schemes [[a,b,c,c,d,d,e,e],[f,f,g,g,h,h,i,i]]
Number of Different Rhyme Schemes 2
Multiplier Factor 3.5
Different Stanzas RSs [8]
Different Rhyme Types [4,5]

6.6 SPARSAR Linguistic and Statistic Graphical Modeling

Eventually, the system produces seven complex indices which include a final best grading index to evaluate a poem in comparison with others. These indices allow comparison amongst a number of poems by the same or different authors, and the selection of the two poems which are the closest according to the indices computed.

SPARSAR visualizes differences by increasing the length and the width of the coloured bars. Here below is the output of the system for two poems "Bells" and "A Death at Winson Green". Parameters evaluated are shown by coloured bars and include: Poetic Rhetoric Devices (in red); Metrical Length (in green); Semantic Density (in blue); Prosodic Structure Dispersion (in black); Deep Conceptual Index (in brown); Rhyming Scheme Comparison (in purple). Their extension indicates the dimension and size of the index: longer bars are for higher values. In this way it is easily shown which component of the poem has major weight in the evaluation. Two poems are then easily comparable visually in that manner, as can be seen from the two figures below, Figs. 6 and 7, where the two poems indicated are shown.

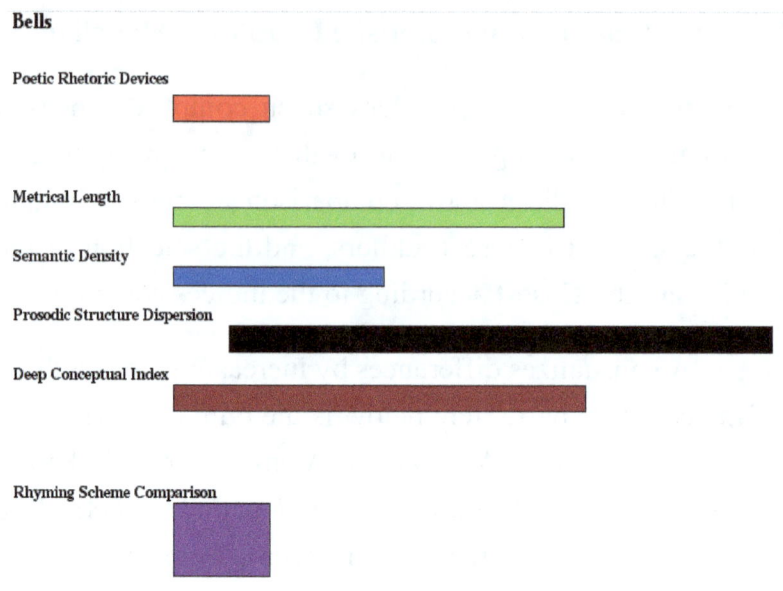

Figure 6. *Sparsar* Indices for the poem Bells

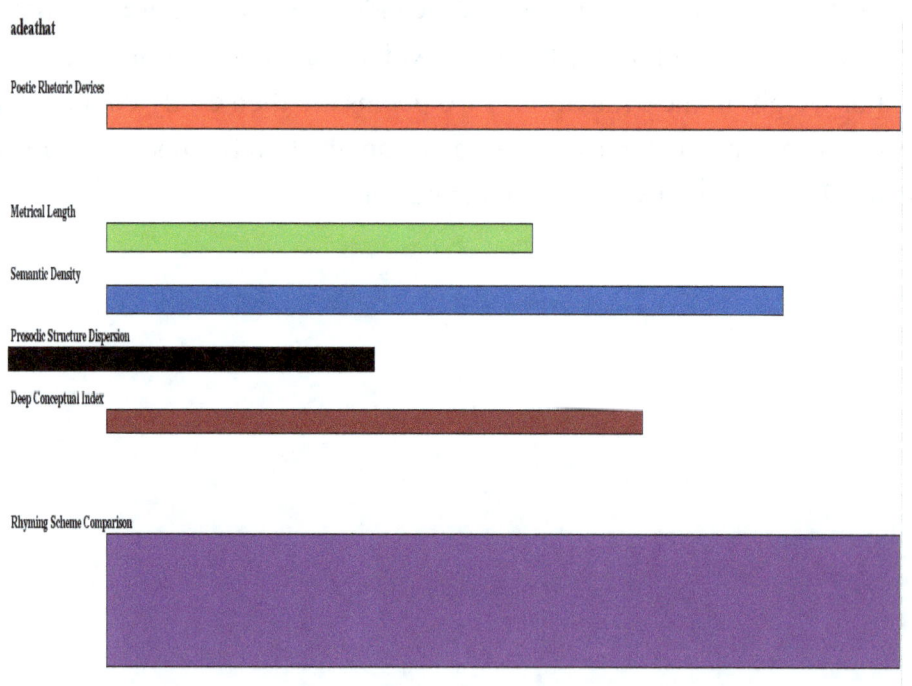

Figure 7. SPARSAR Indices for the poem A Death at Winson Green

In the figures below we show comparisons of different poems by the same author as we did using APSA system. In our case, the representation is two dimensional rather than one dimensional as in APSA where the position in space indicates conformity or deviancy as would cluster analysis. We use size of the box to indicate the importance of the different indices: the bigger the size the more important and the higher score they have got. Position in space on the contrary is used to indicate distributional properties of the different indices: if the indices are well balanced then the position would be center otherwise it would move sideways. This movement is determined by values computed from Skewness and Kurtosis indices and are basically related to Standard Deviation. As can be gather from the position of Five Days Old, it is computed as central also in our space, but the remaining poems are all scattered in different positions from what APSA did.

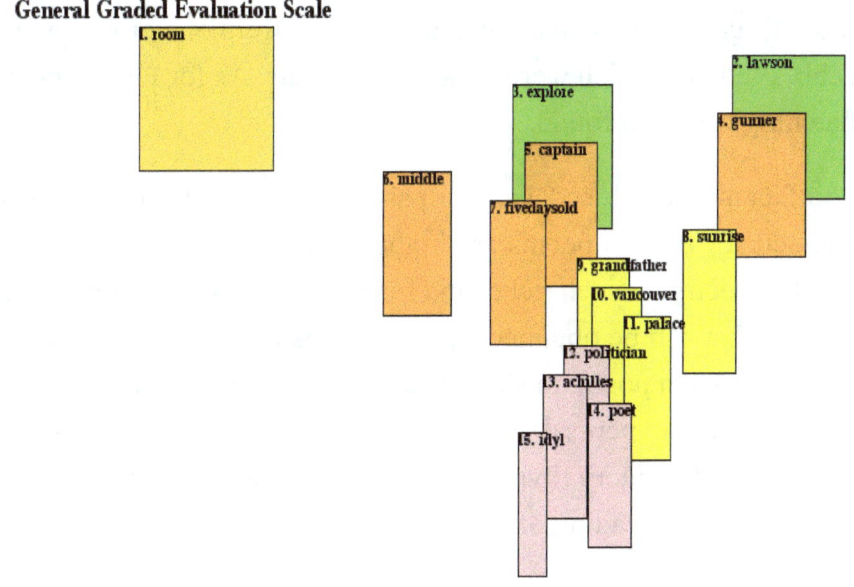

Figure 8. SPARSAR Indices for 15 deviant poems according to APSA

In particular, in our figure 8 a poem like *To a Poet* is positioned at the bottom rather than at the top as in APSA, and *The Explorer's Wife* is positioned at the top rather than at the bottom. Also *The Gunner* is in high position and not in a low position. The same applies to *A Sunrise*. In other words we have totally different appraisal of the content of the poems in the two systems.

6.6.1 Comparing two poets: Webb and Plath

As a final exercise, I computed the comparative image of 53 poems by Sylvia Plath and the same amount by Francis Webb. This should result in a general image which is suggestive of the way in which the poetic world has been organized as a whole. The spread of the poems in the space is much wider in Plath's figure than in Webb's. I computed the same poems with APSA tool – which we don't show here - and didn't get any valuable comparison apart from one or two poems in Webb's scheme which were regarded deviants. As for Plath's poems no matching has been found.

In fact all the values – we don't show them here for lack of space - computed for Plath's poems are higher than Webb's thus indicating that Plath's poetry is much richer and more consistent than Webb's. But of course, what can be obtained by these measurements is only part of the content of each poem: metaphors and images can only be evaluated by critical manual perusal of each stanza and each line. Also the intermingling of imagery rhyme and rhythm can only be appreciated by deep and profound reading of the poems.

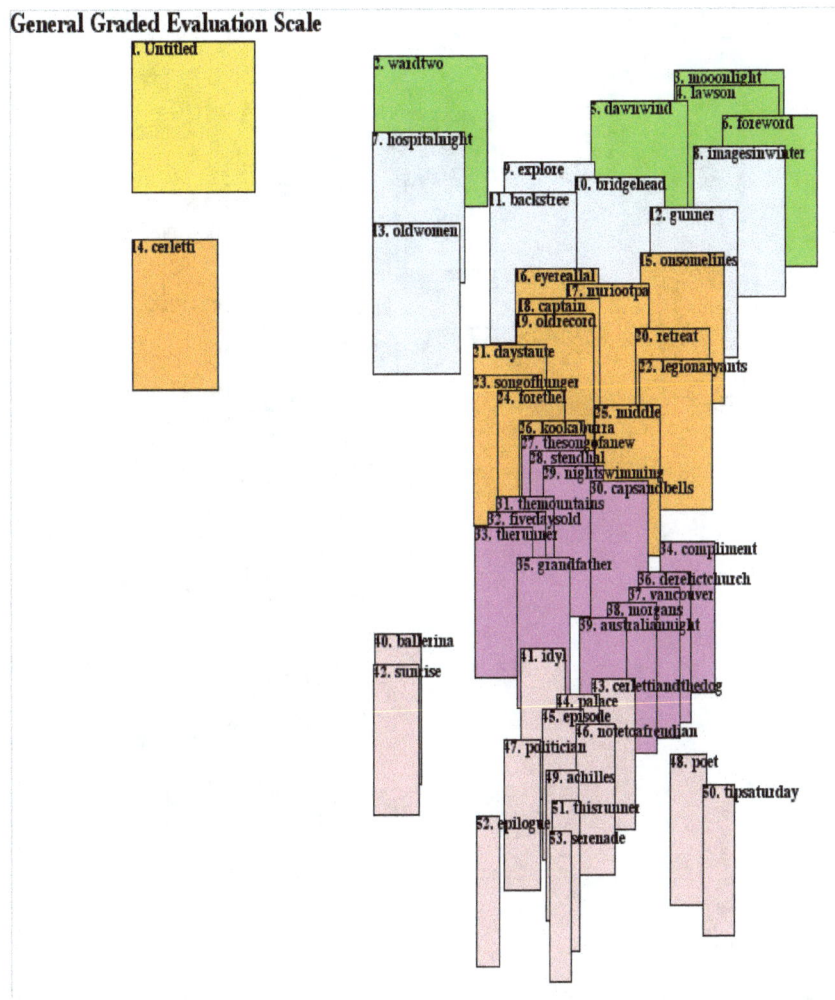

Figure 9. SPARSAR General Graded Evaluation of 53 poems by Webb

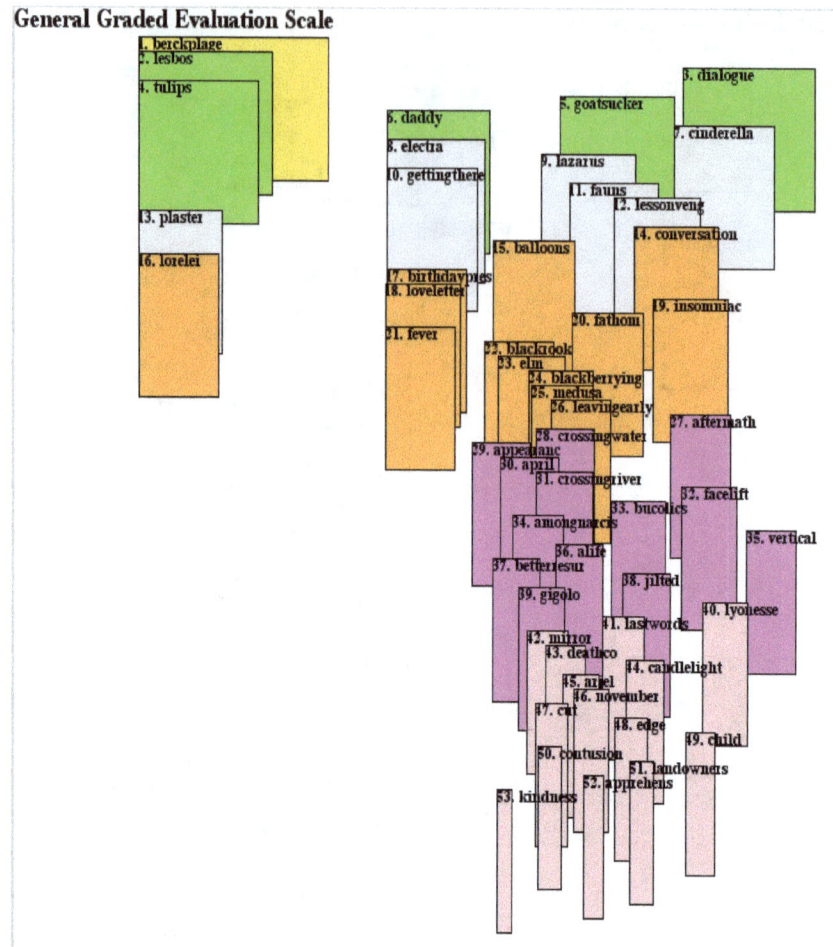

Figure 10. SPARSAR General Graded Evaluation of 53 poems by Plath

Another important feature of the system is the possibility to compare the works of two poets and to receive as a result the closest two poems if any such poem has been so evaluated by the system. Using the six macro indices to measure the semantic and prosodic content of each poem, the system is able at the end of the computation to make comparisons and this is done by transforming into correlation coefficients each pair of macro indices associated to any two poems from the list of the two authors to be compared. We use the formula for

Pearson's correlation coefficients. Here below are th best correlations coefficients obtained from a comparison of the most similar poems chosen from Francis Webb and Sylvia Plath collected poems:

Nessun Dorma - Blackberrying: 0.9995063248666134
A Death at W.G - The old women: 0.9983739250672603
A Death at W.G - Blackberrying: 0.9978765513783355
The Explorer's Wife - Blackberrying: 0.9970534742059991
Nessun Dorma – The old women: 0.9964034793378926
On first hearing - Dialogue between: 0.992759946803719
A Death at W.G – The Goatsucker: 0.9925550806997867
Nessun Dorma – The Goatsucker: 0.9923992745484463
The Explorer's Wife – The old women: 0.9903907589788684

And here below are the two graphical representations for the two best choices Nessun Dorma and Blackberrying, where we can see that the correlation coefficients measure take really close shots of actual values computed by the system.

Figure 11. SPARSAR evaluation for Plath's poem Blackberrying

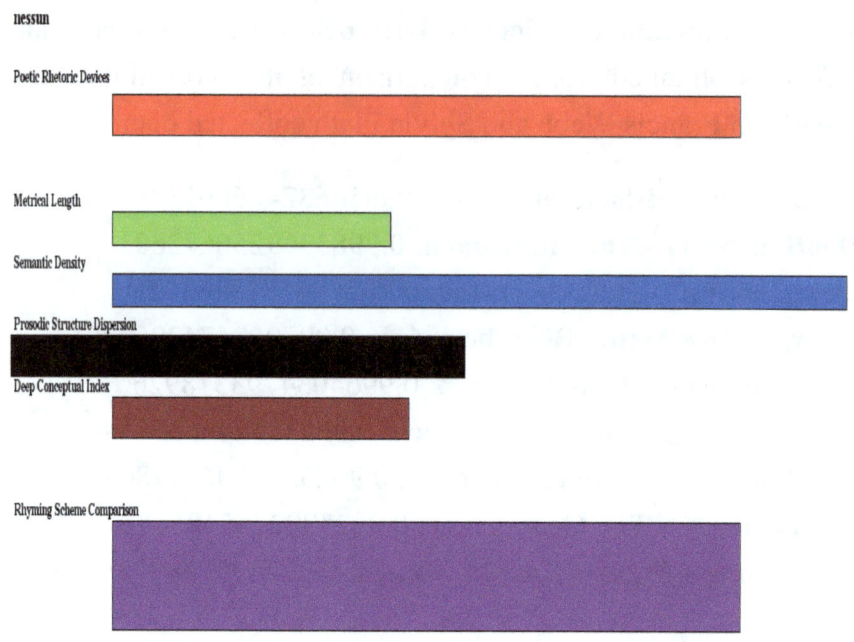

Figure 12. SPARSAR evaluation for Webb's poem Nessun Dorma

Comparisons between two or more poets can also be obtained using APSA and the immediate visual result is a number of scattered coloured labels around the central cloud cluster. I will show here below a set of comparisons between the most important poets of last century and Francis Webb and make comments only on the outliers.

In Figure 13 we show comparison between Webb and Plath poetry, where the latter is projected with yellow colour.

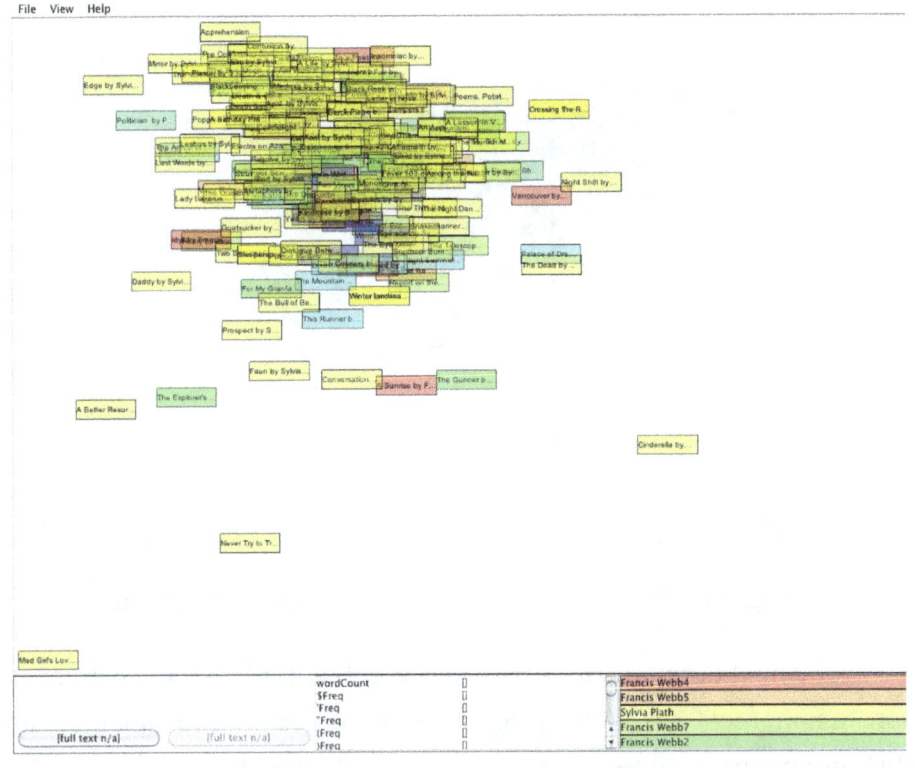

Figure 13. Comparison between Plath and Webb using APSA

And as can be visually gathered, Plath's poems are the only outliers.

6.6.2 Comparing Webb with more poets

In the following figure I show comparison between Webb and Emily Dickinson, where again we see how Webb's poetry is more consistently organized: the only outliers belong to Dickinson's poetry.

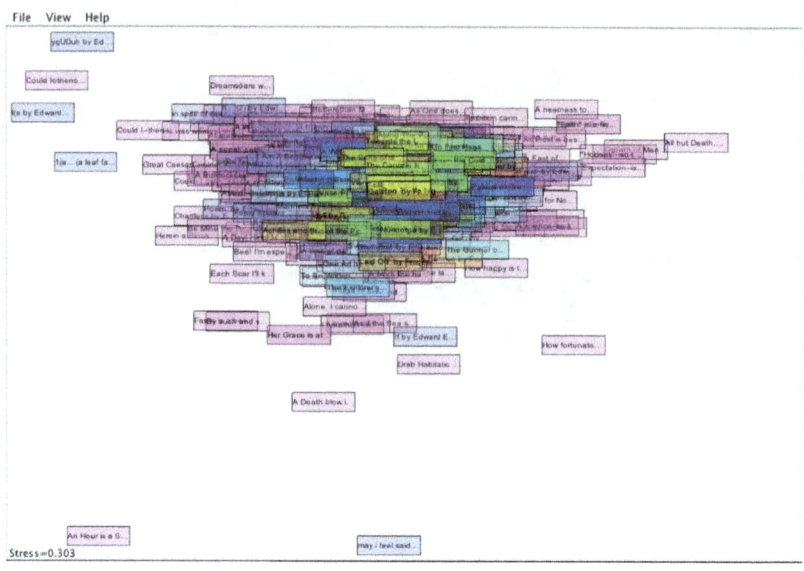

Figure 14. Webb and Dickinson's poetry compared

The next comparison is between Webb and Elizabeth Bishop, and here again most of Webb's poetry is included in the inner cluster. Bishop's poetry is represented using a faint blue colour.

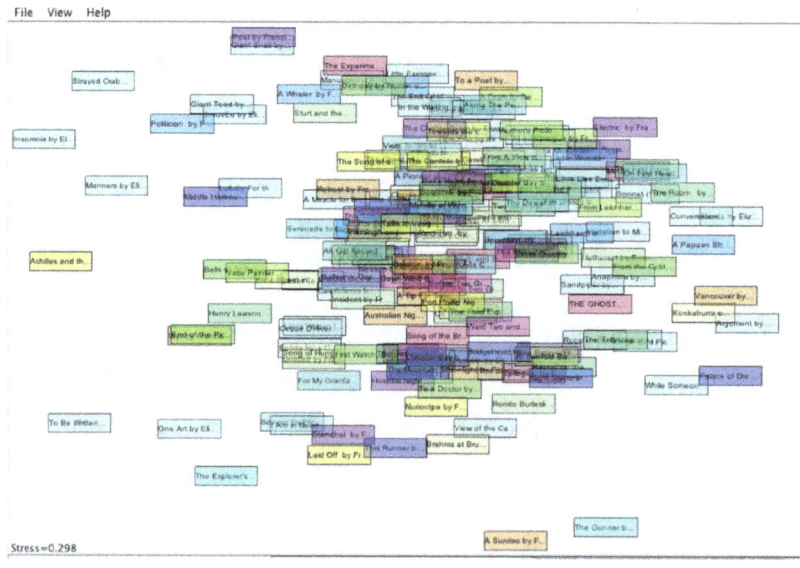

Figure 15. Comparison between Webb and Bishop's poetry

As can be noted, the similarities between the two poets are much more evident and the outliers include also some of Webb's poems. The whole picture is a combination of poems by the two poets even though the central part being more colourful is clearly occupied by Webb. Finally, a comparison between two male poets, Webb and Edward Estling Cummings, where we see how much different two poets may be.

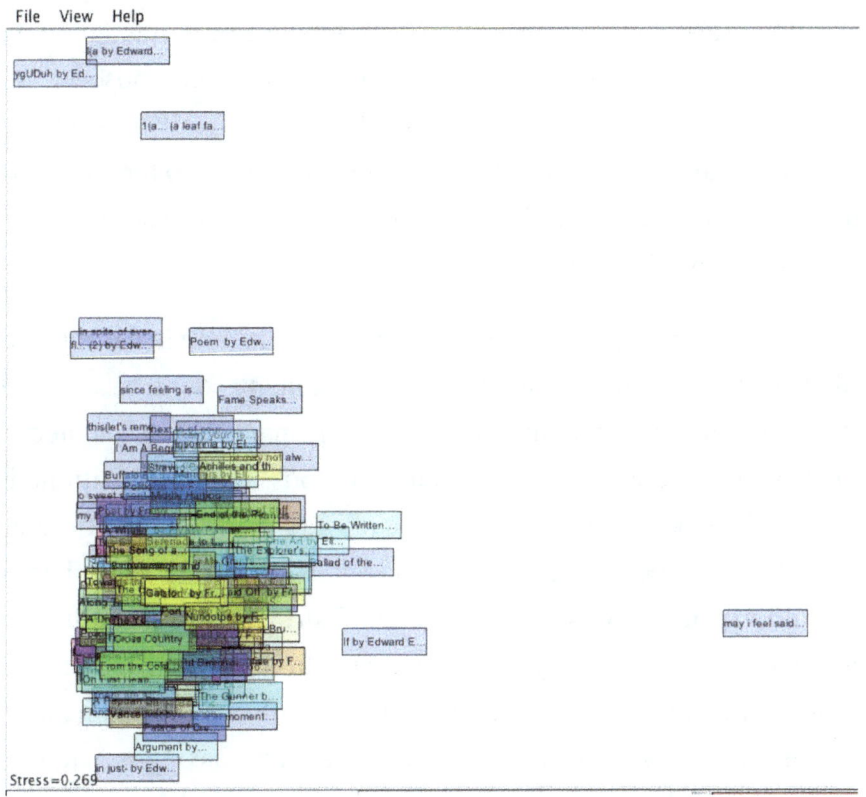

Figure 16. Comparison between E.E. Cummings and Webb

As can be noticed, all of Webb's poetry is included in the cluster central cloud and outliers can be found in almost all directions, but they all belong to Cummings. So eventually we may affirm that Webb's poetry is consistently similar to Bishop's poetry, and only slightly similar to the other three poets considered, regarding Cummings poetry as the one more aloof from Webb's poetry.

6.8 Sound and Sense Harmony

In this final section I will introduce another type of graphical maps this time highlighting differences using colours associated to sound and sense alone (see Kao & Jurafsky, 2012). The use of colours associated to sound in poetry has a long tradition. Rimbaud composed a poem devoted to "Vowels" where colours where specifically associated to each of the main five vowels. Roman Jakobson wrote extensively about sound and colour in a number of papers (Jakobson1; Jakobson2:188), lately papers by Mazzeo.

As Tsur notes, Fónagy wrote an article in which he connected explicitly the use of certain types of consonant sound associated to certain moods: unvoiced and obstruent consonants are associated with aggressive mood; sonorants with tender moods. Fónagy mentioned the work of M.Macdermott who in her study identified a specific quality associated to "dark" vowels, i.e. back vowels, that of being linked with dark colours, mystic obscurity, hatred and struggle. As a result, we are using darker colours to highlight back and front vowels as opposed to low and middle vowels, the latter with light colours. The same applies to representing unvoiced and obstruent consonants as opposed to voiced and sonorants. But as Tsur (see Tsur:15) notes, this sound-colour association with mood or attitude has no real significance without a link to semantics.

In the Semantic Relational View, we are using dark colours for Concrete referents vs Abstract ones with lighter colours; dark colours also for Negatively marked words as opposed to Positively marked ones with lighter colours. The same strategy applies to other poetic maps: this technique has certainly the good quality of highlighting opposing differences at some level of abstraction[44].

With this experiment I intend to verify the number of poems in Webb's corpus in which it is possible to establish a relationship between semantic content in terms of negative vs positive sense - usually referred to with one word as "the sentiment"[45] - and the sound produced by syllables in particular, stressed ones. I assume that it is possible to regard vowel and consonant sounds as carrier of a sensation inducing a sad rather than a happy feeling in the reader. Thus, I will match negative sentiment expressed by the words' sense with sad sounding rhymes and poetic devices as a whole, and the opposite for positive sentiment by scoring and computing the ratios.

In particular, I organized vowel sounds into four main classes:

- Low, Middle, High-Front, High-Back
  where I identify the two classes Low and Middle as promoting positive feelings, and the two High as inducing negative ones.

As to the consonants, I organized the sounds into three main classes and two types:

- *Obstruents* (Plosives, Affricates), *Continuants* (Fricatives), *Sonorants* (Liquids, Vibrants, Approximants)

plus

---

[44] our approach is not comparable to work by Saif Mohammad, where colours are associated to words on the basis of what their mental image may suggest to the mind of annotators hired via Mechanical Turk. The resource only contains word-colour association for some 12,000 entries over the 27K items listed. It is however comparable to a long list of other attempts at depicting phonetic differences in poems as will be discussed further on.
[45] see in particular Brysbaert et al. 2014 that has a database of 40K entries. We are also using a manually annotated lexicon of 10K entries and WordNet supersenses. We are not using MRCDatabase which only has some 8,000 concrete + some 9,000 imagery classified entries because it is difficult to adapt and integrate into our system.

- Voiced vs Unvoiced

In this case the ratios are computed dividing the sum of Continuants and Sonorants by number of Obstruents; and the second parameter will be the ratio obtained by dividing number of Voiced by Unvoiced. So eventually, whenever the value of the ratios are above 1, positive results are obtained, the contrary applies whenever values are below 1.

The representation of the proposed Harmony between Sense and Sound will be cast on the usual vector space where I organized the space as follows:

- Class A:
  Negatively harmonic poems, mainly negatively marked poems on the left. Either the sounds or the sentiment are in majority negative, or both the sounds and the sentiment are negative;
- Class C.
  Positively harmonic poems, mainly positively marked poems on the right. Either the sounds or the sentiment are in majority positive, or both the sounds and the sentiment are positive;
- Class B
  Disharmonic ones in the middle. The sounds and the sentiment have opposite values and either one or the other have values below a given threshold.

In addition to the evaluation of positive/negative values we consider the two parameters we already computed related to Metrical Length and Rhyming Scheme that we add together and use for its 10% added value to compensate for poetic relevant features.

With this experiment we also intend to test the hypothesis cast by the results obtained with the system made available by D.Kaplan, which gave a list of "deviant" poems, and also the results obtained by the overall similar parameters used by our system where deviant poems did not coincide with the ones produced by the analysis made with APSA.

As we saw previously, the following poems were regarded "deviant" and they are:

A Sunrise, The Gunner, The Explorer's Wife, For
My Grandfather, Idyll, Middle Harbour, Politician, To a Poet,
The Captain of the Oberon, Palace of Dreams, The Room,
Vancouver by Rail, Henry Lawson, Achilles and the Woman.

On the contrary, the poem that best represented balanced values was *Five Days Old* which occupied the centre of the figure. Here below in Fig. 17 we present the result of our experiments starting from the 15 poems mentioned above and then showing more output from the system SPARSAR.

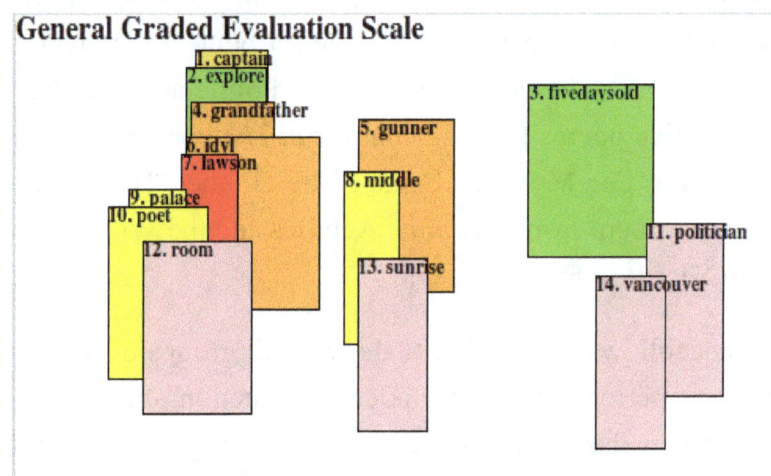

Figure 17. Poems considered as Deviants Evaluated for their degree of Sense/Sound Harmony

The figure shows which poems achieved harmonic values and positioned positives on the right and negative on the left sides, and then in the middle the disharmonic ones. As clearly appears, "Five Days Old", "Politician" and "Vancouver by Rail" are the three poems computed as endowed with positive harmony, while the remaining poems are either characterized as strongly negative - "Poet", "Palace of Dreams" and "The Room" - or just negative, "The Captain of the Oberon", The Explorer's Wife", "For My Grandfather", "Idyll", and "Henry Lawson". Finally the last three poems positioned in the centre left are disharmonic, "The Gunner", "Middle Harbour", and "A Sunrise", where disharmonic means that the parameters of Sounds are in opposition to those of Sense. Slight variations in the position are determined by the contribution of parameters computed from poetic devices as said above. Disharmony as will be discussed further on might be regarded as a choice by the poet with the intended aim to reconcile the opposites in the poem.

The choice of these 15 poems includes poetry written at the beginning of the career, i.e. included in the *Early Poems* - A Sunrise, Palace of Dreams, To a Poet, Idyll, Middle Harbour, Vancouver by Rail -; two poems from *A Drum for Ben Boyd*, - Politician, The Captain of the Oberon -; five poems from *Leichhardt in Theatre* - The Room, The Explorer's Wife, For My Grandfather, The Gunner, Henry Lawson-; and finally one poem from *Birthday,* Achilles and the Woman, and one poem from *Socrates*, Five Days Old.

In what follows, at first I will show small groups of poems taken from different periods in Webb's poetic production and discuss them separately, rather than conflating them all in a single image. In fact at the end of this section I will show a bigger picture where I analysed together 87 poems thus resulting in two big figures. Back to the second experiment where I collected and analyzed the following poems:

Early Poems
Idyll, The Mountains, Vancouver by Rail, A Tip for Saturday, This

Runner

Leichhardt in Theatre
Melville at Woods Hole, For Ethel, On First Hearing a Cuckoo

Poems 1950-52
The Runner, Nuriootpa

Birthday
Ball's Head Again, The Song of a New Australian

Socrates
The Yellowhammer

The Ghost of the Cock
Ward Two and the Kookaburra

Unfinished Works
Episode, Untitled

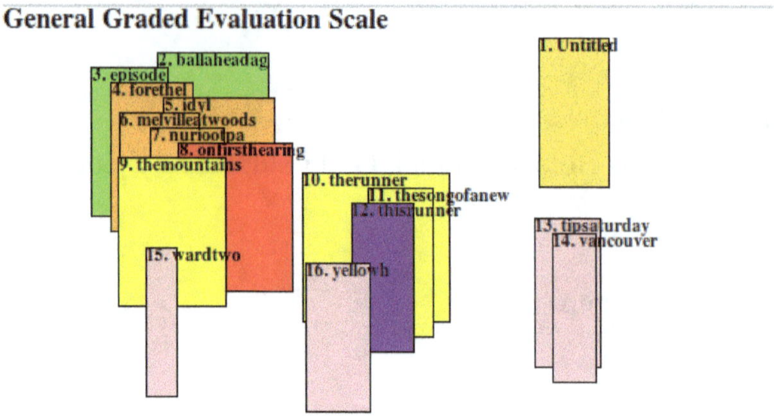

General Graded Evaluation Scale

Figure 18. Sixteen poems from different periods of Webb's poetic production computed for their Sense/Sound Harmony

Here again it is important to notice the majority of the poems positioned on the left hand side thus analyzed as possessing negative harmony; only three poems on the right hand side, one of which is the unfinished "Untitled". And then in the middle a small number of disharmonic poems, or we could call them poems in which there were conflicting forces contributing to the overall meaning intended by the poem.

Also take into account the dimension of the box which signal the major or minor contribution of the overall parameters computed as discussed in previous section, of all the linguistic and poetic features contained in the poem, but measured on the basis of their minor or major dispersion using Standard Deviation.

In the following group I added more poems from later work, which were computer mainly as positive:

Birthday
Hopkins and Foster's Dam

Socrates
A Death at Winson Green

Eyre All Alone
Bells of St Peter Mancroft

The Ghost of the Cock
Around Costessey
Nessun Dorma

Late Poems 1969-73
Lament for St Maria Goretti
St Therese and the Child

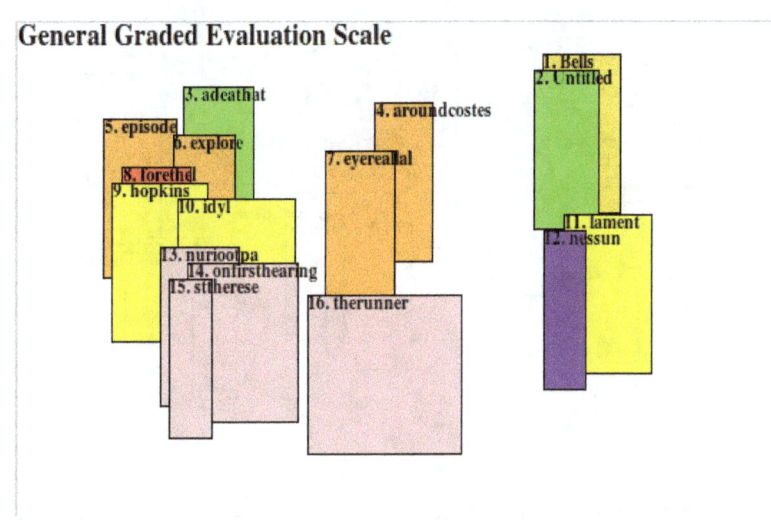

Figure 19. Sixteen poems taken mainly from late poetic production computed for their Sense/Sound Harmony

I am now showing a bigger picture containing 50 poems, where we can see again the great majority of them being positioned on the left hand side. The positive side is enriched by "Moonlight" from *Early Poems*, and "Song of the Brain" from *Socrates*, and the middle disharmonic list now counts 16 poems.

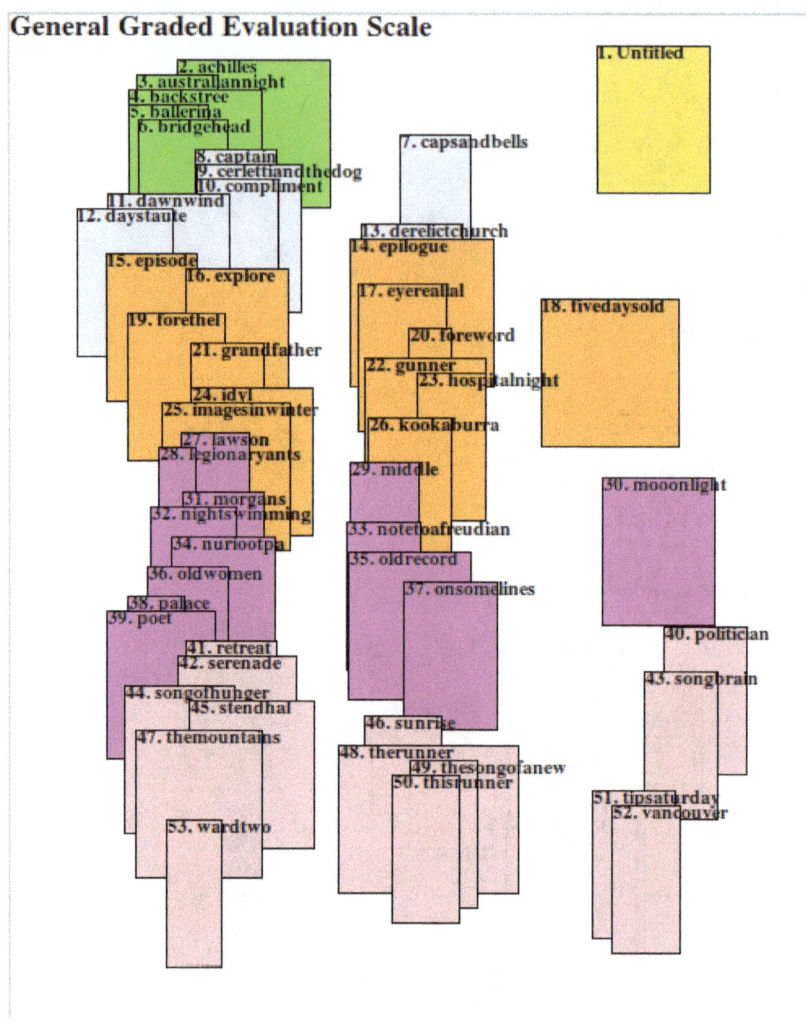

Figure 20. Fifty Poems computed by Sense/Sound Harmony

So we can safely say that the great majority of Webb's poems contain a negative harmony. This is further confirmed by the following figure which represents the analysis of 87 poems, I decided not to increase the number of poems up to 130 as was done with APSA system simply because otherwise the image becomes too difficult to read and poems' labels will be too cluttered together.

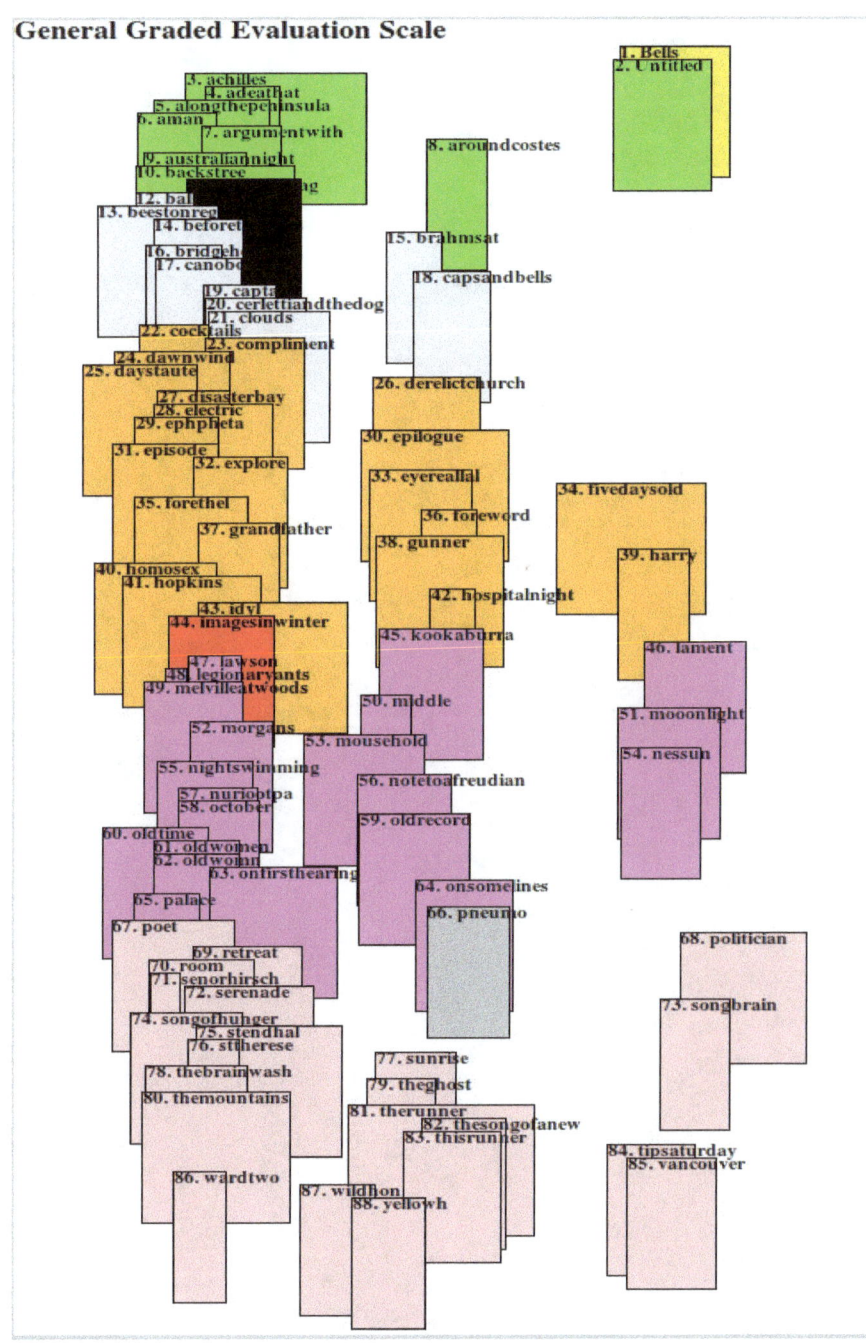

Figure 21. Sound Sense Harmony in Webb's 87 poems

BIBLIOGRAPHY

On Poetry

Eliot, T.S: 1970. Four Quartets, London; 1st ed. 1944.

Lawrence, D.H.: 1964. The Complete Poems, 2 voll., London.

Yeats, W.B.: 1973. Collected Poems, London.

Yeats, W.B.: 1937. A Vision, London.

Buckley, Vincent. 1957. Essay on Poetry - Mainly Australian, Clarendon.

Buckley, Vincent, 1968. Poetry and the Sacred, London.

Genette, Gerard. 1967. Figures II, Paris.

Green, H.M. 1961. A History of Australian Literature, 2 voll. Sydney.

Guiraud, Pierre. 1969. Essays de stylistique, Paris.

Jakobson, Roman. 1974. Question de poétique, Paris.

Jeffares, Norman. 1968. A Commentary on the Collected Poems of W.B.Yeats, London.

Kristeva, Julia. 1974. La révolution du langage poétique, Paris.

Miles, J.. Major adjectives in English poetry: from Wyatt to Auden. University of California Publications in English, 12(3):305–426, 1946.

Miles, J. (1967). Style and Proportion: The Language of Prose and Poetry. Little, Brown and Co., Boston.

Modern American Poetry. (2002). Ed. Cary Nelson. U. of Illinois at Urbana-Champaign. http://www.english.uiuc.edu/maps.

Read, Herbert. 1969. "Introduction" to Francis Webb, Collected Poems, Sydney, 1969.

Oxford Anthology of Modern American Poetry. (2000). Ed. Cary Nelson. Oxford U. Press. OUP online U.S. General Catalog. 2005. http://www.us.oup.com /us/catalog/general/subject/?view =usa&sf=toc&ci= 0195122712.

Poetry of the United States. http://en.wikipedia.org/wiki/Poetry_ of_the _United _States.

Ruwet, Nicolas. 1972. Langage, musique, poésie, Paris.

Twelve Poets, 1950-70, edited by A.Craig, Milton, 1971.

Ullman, Stephen. 1968. Stile e linguaggio, Firenze.

Webb Francis, 1969. Collected Poems, Angus and Robertson, Sydney & London.

Wilkes, G.A. 1969. Australian Literature: A Conspectus, Sydney.

Wright, Judith, 1965. Preoccupations in Australian Poetry, Melbourne.

On Literature, Myth, Symbolism, Anthropology

Bidney, David, 1958. Anthropological Thought, in The Philosophy of Ernst Cassirer, ed. by H.Schlipp, New York.

Bodkin, Maud, 1971. Archetypal Patterns in Poetry, Psychological Studies of Imagination, Oxford.

Bodkin, Maud, 1951. Studies on Type-Images, Oxford.

Bowra, C.M., 1968. Landmarks in Greek Literature, Penguin.

Delmonte Rodolfo, 1977. "Myth, Creativity and Society in the Poetry of James McAuley, A.D.Hope, Francis Webb", Unpub. Ph.D. Dissertation, Monash University.

Docker, John, 1974. Australian Cultural Elites, Sydney.

Frye, Northrop, 1964. The Educated Imagination, Bloomington.

The Homeric Hymns, transl. by C.Boer, Chicago, 1970.

Iesi, Furio, 1968. Letteratura e Mito, Torino.

Jameson, Frederic, 1971. Marxism and Form: Twentieth-Century Dialectical Theories of Literature, Princeton.

Langer, K.S., "Theory of Language and Myth", in The Philosophy of Ernest Cassirer, cit.

Lilar, Suzanne, 1965. Aspects of Love - in Western Society, London.

Melchiori, Giorgio, 1956. The Tightrope Walkers, London.

Miller, J.H., 1966. Poets of Reality, Cambridge Mass.

Moore, V. 1954. The Unicorn; W.B.Yeats' Search for Reality, New York.

Paz, Octavio, 1971. Claude Levi-Strauss: An Introduction, London.

Piro, Sergio, 1967. Il linguaggio schizofrenico, Milano.

Tindall, M.V., 1950. James Joyce - His Way of Interpreting the World, New York.

Trilling, Lionel, 1970. The Liberal Imagination, Essays on Literature and Society, Pelican Books.

Tynjanov, Jurij, 1929. Arachaisty i novatory, Leningrad.

Vickery, J.B., 1966. Myth and Literature - Contemporary Theory and Practice, Lincoln.

Whalley, G. 1953. Poetic Process, London.

On Psychology and Creativity

Arnheim, Rudolph, 1966. Towards a Psychology of Art, London.

Baynes, H.G., 1969. Mythology of the Soul - A Research into the Unconscious from Schizophrenic Dreams and Drawings, London.

Bergler, Edmund, 1950. The Writer and Psychoanalysis, New York.

Chasseguet-Smirgel, J., 1971. Pour une psychoanalyse de l'art et de la créativité, Paris.

Cooper, David, 1972. Psychiatry and Antipsychiatry, Paladin.

Cooper, David, 1972. The Death of the Family, Pelican Books.

Crowcroft, A., 1968. The Psychotic, Understanding Madness, Penguin Books.

Dominian, J. 1962. Psychiatry and the Christian, London.

Erikson, E., 1966. Identity, Youth and Crisis, New York.

Fairbairn, W.R.D., 1952. Psychoanalytic Studies of the Personality, London.

Freud, Sigmund, Collected Works, London;

"Delusion and Dreams in Jensen's Gradive", 9th vol., 1959.

"Dostoevsky and Parricide", 21st vol., 1961.

"Creative Writers and Day-Dreaming", 9th vol., 1959.

Fromm, Erick, 1951. The Forgotten Language - An Introduction to the Understanding of Dreams, Fairy Tales and Myths, New York.

Fry, Roger, 1924. The Artist and Psycho-Analysis. London.

Fry, Roger, 1947. Psychoanalysis and Art, New York.

Gombrick, E.H., 1960. The Story of Art, London.

Guntrip, Harry, 1968. Schizoid Phenomena, Object-Relations and the Self. London.

Guntrip, Harry, 1961. Personality Structure and Human Interaction, London.

Jung, C.G., Collected Works, New York;

- The Development of Personality, 17th vol., 1964.

- Psychology and Religion - West and East, 2nd vol., 1964.

- Symbols of Transformation, 5th vol., 1956.

Krist, Ernest, 1953. Psychoanalytic Explorations in Art, London.

Laing, R.D., 1965. The Divided Self, Penguin Books.

Laing, R.D., 1971. Self and Others, Pelican Books.

Laing, R.D. and A.Esterton, 1972. Sanity, Madness and the Family,

Pelican Books.

Mannoni, Octave, 1963. Clefs pour l'Imaginaire ou l'Autre Scène, Paris.

Mauron, Charles, 1953. Aesthetics and Psychology, London.

Mauron, Charles, 1963. Introduction à la psychanalyse de Mallarmé, Neuchatel.

Mauron, Charles, 1963. Des Métaphors obsédantes au Mythe personel, Paris.

Neumann, Erich, 1969. Art and the Creative Unconscious, London.

New Directions in Psychoanalysis Today, ed. by Melanie Klein, London, 1955; essays by Hanna Segal, Paula Heinemann, W.R.Bion et alia.

Plokker, J.H., 1964. Artistic Self-Expression in Mental Disease, - The Shattered Image of Schizophrenics, London.

Storr, Antony, 1972. The Dynamics of Creation, New York.

Szatz, T.S., 1972. The Myth of Mental Illness, Paladin.

Winnicott, D.W., 1958. Collected Papers: "Through Pediatrics to Psycho-Analysis, London.

Computational and Quantitative Linguistics

Alfie Abdul-Rahman, Julie Lein, Katharine Coles, Eamonn Maguire, Miriah Meyer, and Martin Wynne, Chris Johnson, Anne E. Trefethen, Min Chen. 2013. Rule-based Visual Mappings - with a Case Study on Poetry Visualization. In Computer Graphics

Forum, 32(3):381-390.

Agirrezabal Manex, Bertol Arrieta, Aitzol Astigarraga, Mans Hulden, 2013. POS-tag based poetry generation with WordNet, Proceedings of the 14th European Workshop on Natural Language Generation, pages 162–166.

M. Agirrezabal, B. Arrieta, A. Astigarraga, M. Hulden. 2013. "ZeuScansion: a tool for scansion of English poetry," Proceedings of the 11th International Conference on Finite State Methods and Natural Language Processing.

Algee-Hewitt, M., Heuser, R. Kraxenberger, M., Porter, J., Sensenbaugh, J., and Tackett, J. (2014). The Stanford Literary Lab Transhistorical Poetry Project Phase II: Metrical Form. Proceedings, Stanford University, Lausanne.

Apresjan, D.Juri, 1973. Principles and Methods of Contemporary Structural Linguistics, The Hague.

Baayen R. H., R. Piepenbrock, and L. Gulikers. 1995. The CELEX Lexical Database (CD-ROM). Linguistic Data Consortium.

Bacalu C., Delmonte R. (1999). Prosodic Modeling for Syllable Structures from the VESD - Venice English Syllable Database, in Atti 9° Convegno GFS-AIA, Venezia.

Susan Bartlett, Grzegorz Kondrak, and Colin Cherry. 2009. On the syllabification of phonemes. In Proceedings of Human Language Technologies: NAACL '09. ACL, Stroudsburg, PA, USA, 308-316.

Brysbaert, M., Warriner, A.B., & Kuperman, V. 2014. Concreteness ratings for 40 thousand generally known English word lemmas. Behavior Research Methods, 46, 904-911.

Byrd Roy J. and M. S. Chodorow. 1985. Using an online dictionary to find rhyming words and pronunciations for unknown words. In Proceedings of the 23rd Annual Meeting of ACL, 277–283.+

Bacalu C., Delmonte R. (1999), Prosodic Modeling for Speech Recognition, in Atti del Workshop AI*IA - "Elaborazione del Linguaggio e Riconoscimento del Parlato", IRST Trento, pp.45-55.

Delmonte R.(1979), Piercing into the Psyche: the Poetry of Francis Webb - with a Select Concordance of Keywords and Keyroots, CETID, Venezia.

Delmonte R. (1980). Computer Assisted Literary Textual Analysis with Keymorphs and Keyroots, REVUE-Informatique et Statistique dans les Sciences humaines,1, 21-53.

Delmonte R. (1983). A Quantitative Analysis of Linguistic Deviation: Francis Webb, a Schizophrenic Poet, in REVUE – Informatique et Statistique dans les Sciences humaines, 19:1-4, 55-112.

Delmonte R., et al. 2005. VENSES – a Linguistically-Based System for Semantic Evaluation, in J. Quiñonero-Candela et al.(eds.), Machine Learning Challenges. LNCS, Springer, Berlin, 344-371.

Delmonte, R., (2010), Prosodic tools for language learning, International Journal of Speech Technology. Volume 12 Number 4, pp.161 – 184.

Delmonte R. and V. Pallotta, 2011. Opinion Mining and Sentiment Analysis Need Text Understanding, in "Advances in Distributed Agent-based Retrieval Tools", Springer, 81-96.

Delmonte R. (2013). SPARSAR: a System for Poetry Automatic Rhythm and Style AnalyzeR, SLATE 2013, Demonstration

Track.

Delmonte R. (2013), Transposing Meaning into Immanence: The Poetry of Francis Webb, in Rivista di Studi Italiani, Vol. XXX1, n° 1, 835-892.

Delmonte R. & A.M. Prati. 2014. SPARSAR: An Expressive Poetry Reader, Proceedings of the Demonstrations at the 14th Conference of the EACL, Gotheborg, 73–76.

Delmonte R. 2014. ITGETARUNS A Linguistic Rule-Based System for Pragmatic Text Processing, in C. Bosco, P. Cosi, F. Dell'Orletta, M. Falcone, S. Montemagni, Maria Simi (eds.), Proceedings of Fourth International Workshop EVALITA, Pisa University Press, Vol. 2, 64-69.

Rodolfo Delmonte, 2015. Visualizing Poetry with SPARSAR - Poetic Maps from Poetic Content, Proceedings of NAACL-HLT Fourth Workshop on Computational Linguistics for Literature, Denver, Colorado, June 4, 2015. c 2015 Association for Computational Linguistics, pages 68–78.

Delmonte R., 2015. SPARSAR - Expressivity in TTS and its Relations to Semantics, Invited Talk at AISV 2015, Bologna.

Rodolfo Delmonte, 2016. Sparsar recita Shakespeare, SLI-GSCP 2016, Napoli.

R.Delmonte (2016), Expressivity in TTS from Semantics and Pragmatics, in Vayra, M., Avesani, C. & Tamburini F. (Eds.) (2015). Il farsi e disfarsi del linguaggio. Acquisizione, mutamento e destrutturazione della struttura sonora del linguaggio/Language acquisition and language loss. Acquisition, change and disorders of the language sound structure, Milano: AISV. pp. 407-427.

DOI: 10.17469/O2101AISV000026

Rodolfo Delmonte, Cognitive Models of Poetry Reading, Chapter, in Marcel Danesi (ed.) Handbook of Cognitive Science, pp. 1083-1120, Springer International Publishing DOI:10.1007/978-3-030-44982-7_19-4

Rodolfo Delmonte, Introduction to the Section Mathematics and Linguistics. in Marcel Danesi (ed.) Handbook of Cognitive Science, Springer International Publishing.

Fónagy, Iván (1971) "The Functions of Vocal Style", in Seymour Chatman (ed.), Literary Style: A Symposium. London: Oxford UP, 159-174.

Freund, John E., 1967. Modern Elementary Statistics, Englewood Cliffs.

Genzel Dmitriy, J. Uszkoreit, and F. Och. 2010. "Poetic" statistical machine translation: Rhyme and meter. In Proceedings of EMNLP.

Gervás, P. (2001). An expert system for the composition of formal spanish poetry. Knowledge-Based Systems,14(3):181–188.

Gervás, P. (2010). Engineering linguistic creativity: Bird flight and jet planes. In Proceedings of the NAACL HLT 2010 Second Workshop on Computational Approaches to Linguistic Creativity, pages 23–30.

Gladkii, A.V., 1970. Leçons de linguistique mathématique, 2 voll., Paris.

Greene E., T. Bodrumlu, K. Knight. 2010. Automatic Analysis of Rhythmic Poetry with Applications to Generation and

Translation, in Proceedings of the 2010 Conference on EMNLP , 524–533.

Harris, Z.S., 1971. Structures mathématique du language, Paris.

Hartman, C. (2005). The Scandroid Manual. Online + Hartman, C. (2004). Charles Hartman Programs. Online

Hayward, M. (1991). A connectionist model of poetic meter. Poetics, 20, 303-317.

Hayward, M. (1996). Application of a connectionist model of poetic meter to problems in generative metrics. Research in Humanities Computing 4. (pp. 185-192). Oxford: Clarendon Press.

Hays, D.G., 1967. Introduction to Computational Linguistics, New York.

Herdan, G., 1956. Language as a Choice and Chance, Groningen.

Herdan, G. 1971. Linguistica Quantitativa, Bologna.

Herdan, G. 1962. The Calculus of Linguistic Observation, 'S-Gravenhage.

Heuser, R. (2015). Stanford Literary Lab Github Account. Online

Hussein Hirjee and Daniel Brown. 2009. Automatic Detection of Internal and Imperfect Rhymes in Rap Lyrics. In Proceedings of the 10th International Society for Music Information Retrieval Conference. pages 711-716.

Jakobson, R. 1978. Six lectures on sound and meaning (Trans.: J. Mepham). Cambridge: MIT Press (Original work published in 1976).

Jakobson, R., & Waugh, L. 1978. The sound shape of language. Bloomington: Indiana University Press.

Kao Justine and Dan Jurafsky. 2012. A Computational Analysis of Style, Affect, and Imagery in Contemporary Poetry. NAACL Workshop on Computational Linguistics for Literature.

Kaplan, D. (2006). Computational analysis and visualized comparison of style in American poetry. Unpublished undergraduate thesis.

Kaplan, D., & Blei, D. (2007). A computational approach to style in American poetry. In *IEEE Conference on Data Mining*.

Karteek Addanki and Dekai Wu. 2013. Unsupervised Rhyme Scheme Identification in Hip Hop Lyrics using Hidden Markov Models. Proceedings of the 1st International Conference on Statistical Language and Speech Processing (SLSP - 2013), Tarragona, Spain.

Keim D. A., Oelke D.: Literature fingerprinting: A new method for visual literary analysis. In IEEE VAST (2007), pp. 115–122.

Kucera, H., Francis W.N., 1967. Computational Analysis of Present-Day American English. Providence.

McCurdy, Nina, Vivek Srikumar, Miriah Meyer, 2015. RhymeDesign: A Tool for Analyzing Sonic Devices in Poetry, Computational Linguistics for Literature, ACL, Denver, 12-22.

Macdermott M.M. 1940. Vowel Sounds in Poetry: Their Music and Tone Colour, Psyche Monographs, No.13, London: Kegan Paul, 148 pp.

Manish Chaturvedi, Gerald Gannod, Laura Mandell, Helen Armstrong, Eric Hodgson. 2012. Myopia: A Visualization Tool in Support of

Close Reading. Digital Humanities 2012.

Manish Chaturvedi, Gerald Gannod, Laura Mandell, Helen Armstrong, Eric Hodgson. 2012. Rhyme's Challenge: Hip Hop, Poetry, and Contemporary Rhyming Culture. Oxford University Press, Literary Criticism.

Manurung Hisar Maruli, G. Ritchie, and H. Thompson. 2000a. Towards a computational model of poetry generation. In Proceedings of AISB Symposium on Creative and Cultural Aspects and Applications of AI and Cognitive Science, 17-20.

Manurung M.H., G. Ritchie, H. Thompson. 2000b. A Flexible Integrated Architecture For Generating Poetic Texts. in Proceedings of the Fourth Symposium on Natural Language Processing (SNLP 2000), Chiang Mai, Thailand, 7-22.

Mohammad Saif, Colourful Language: Measuring Word-Colour Associations, 2011a. In Proceedings of the ACL 2011 Workshop on Cognitive Modeling and Computational Linguistics (CMCL), June 2011, Portland, OR.

Mohammad Saif, Even the Abstract have Colour: Consensus in Word Colour Associations, 2011b. In Proceedings of the 49th Annual Meeting of the Association for Computational Linguistics: Human Language Technologies, June 2011, Portland, OR.

Mazzeo, M. 2004. Les voyelles colorées: Saussure et la synesthésie. Cahiers Ferdinand de Saussure, 57,129–143.

Mey, J., 1971. Computational Linguistics in the "Seventies'", Linguistics, 74, pp.34-61.

Milic, L.T., 1966. " Computer Approach to Style", in J.Leed(ed.), The Computer and Literary Style, Kent-Ohio.

Oelke D., Bak P., Keim D., Last M., Danon G.: Visual evaluation of text features for document summarization and analysis. In IEEE VAST (Oct. 2008), pp. 75 –82.

Plamondon M. R.: Virtual verse analysis: Analysing patterns in poetry. Literary and Linguistic Computing 21, suppl 1 (2006), 127–141.

Reddy, Sravana & John Goldsmith, 2010. An MDL-based approach to extracting subword units for grapheme-to-phoneme conversion, in Proc. HLT-NAACL, 713-716.

Reddy, Sravana & Kevin Knight. 2011. Unsupervised Discovery of Rhyme Schemes, in Proceedings of the 49th Annual Meeting of ACL: shortpapers, 77-82.

Shutova, E., Teufel S., Korhonen A., 2013. "Statistical Metaphor Processing",in "Computational Linguistics", 39:2, Cambridge Mass., MIT Press.

Sonderegger, Morgan. 2011. Applications of graph theory to an English rhyming corpus. Computer Speech and Language, 25:655–678.

Toivanen, J. M., Toivonen, H., Valitutti, A. & Gross, O. 2012. Corpus-based generation of content and form in poetry. In International Conference on Computational Creativity, 175–179.

Tsur, Reuven. 1992. What Makes Sound Patterns Expressive: The Poetic Mode of Speech-Perception. Durham N. C.: Duke UP.

Tsur Reuven. 2012. Poetic Rhythm: Structure and Performance: An Empirical Study in Cognitive Poetics, Sussex Academic Press, 472.

Wattenberg M., Viégas F. B.: The Word Tree, an interactive visual concordance. IEEE Trans. Visualization & Comp. Graphics 14, 6

(Nov. 2008), 1221–1228.

Wilks V., Charniak, E., (eds.) 1976. Computational Semantics, Amsterdam.

Winograd, T., 1972. Understanding Natural Language, New York.

Zampolli, A., 1970. Fondamenti di linguistica computazionale, Pisa.

Zampolli, A., (ed.) 1977. Linguistic Structure Processing, Amsterdam.

Articles on Francis Webb

Adamson, Robert. "Something Absolutely Splendid." Recorded 24 May 2012. U of Technology, Sydney. Web. 10 Dec.

Ashcroft, W.D., 1974. "The Broads of the Spirit: The Poetry of Francis Webb", Meanjin, 33, 7-18.

Ashcroft, W.D., 1974. "The Storming of the Bastille: The Technique of Francis Webb's Poetry", Southerly, 34, 355-370.

Ashcroft, W.D., 1975. "Centre of Fierceness: Francis Webb's Vision of the Artist", ALS, 12, n.1.

Beaver, Bruce. Letters to Live Poets. Five Dock: South Head Press, 1969.

Beaver, Bruce. "Untitled: review." Sydney Morning Herald (10 May 1969):22.

Brennan, Bernadette. "'Death and the Woman': Looking at Francis Webb's 'Lament for St Maria Goretti.'" Australian Literary Studies 21.3 (2004): 289—98. Print.

Buckley, Vincent, 1970. "The Poetry of Francis Webb", Quadrant, 14, 11-15.

Davidson, Toby. Christian Mysticism and Australian Poetry. New York: Cambria, 2013. Print.

Davidson, Toby."Francis Webb in Western Australia." Westerly 53 (2008): 115—26. Print.

Toby Davidson, 2012. Breath, Laughter, Creation: Launches, Reviews And Errata For Francis Webb Collected Poems.

Davidson, T. (2013). Francis Webb and the 1960s. *Antipodes: a global journal of Australian/New Zealand literature*, *27*(1), 19-24. https://doi.org/10.131 10/antipodes.27.1.0019

Dobson Rosemary, 1974. "Francis Webb", ALS, 6, 227-229.

Griffith, Michael. "Francis Webb and Norman Lindsay." Southerly 49.1 (1989): 32-42. Print.

Griffith, Michael. God's Fool: The Life and Poetry of Francis Webb. North Ryde: Angus and Robertson, 1991. Print.

Griffith, Michael, and James McGlade. Cap and Bells: The Poetry of Francis Webb. North Ryde: Angus and Robertson, 1991. Print.

Hall, Rodney. "Poetry for the converted." The Australian (9 August 1969): 9.

Heseltine, H.P., 1967. "The Very Gimbals of Unease: The Poetry of Francis Webb", Meanjin, 26, 255-274.

Meere, Leonie and Peter Meere, eds. Francis Webb, Poet and Brother: Some of his Letters and Poetry. Pomona: Sage, 2000.

Murray, Les. "Death of a Poet." Sydney Morning Herald (19 January 1974): 15–16.

Poetry Australia, 1975. Francis Webb Commemorative Issue, Number Fifty-six, Sydney.

Powell, Craig. The Nameless Father in the Poetry and Life of Francis Webb. Warners Bay: Picaro, 2008.

Read, Herbert. "Preface." Collected Poems. Francis Webb, author. Sydney: Angus & Robertson, 1969: v–ix.

Wallace-Crabbe, C., 1961. "Order and Turbolence: The Poetry of Francis Webb", Commonwealth Literary Fund Lectures, Charlton.

Webb, Francis. Collected Poems. Toby Davidson, ed. Crawley: University of Western Australia Publishing, 2011.

www.ingramcontent.com/pod-product-compliance
Lightning Source LLC
Chambersburg PA
CBHW072234290426
44111CB00012B/2085